Contents

CONTENTS

Ethnic Minorities in Britain

Sociology and the Modern World
Series Editor: Professor John Rex

Ernest Krausz

Ethnic Minorities in Britain

MacGibbon & Kee London

Granada Publishing Limited
First published in Great Britain 1971 by MacGibbon & Kee Ltd
3 Upper James Street London WIR 4BP

Copyright © 1971 by Ernest Krausz

ISBN 0 261 63241 8
Printed in Great Britain by Cox & Wyman Ltd
London, Fakenham and Reading

Acknowledgements

It is a pleasant task for me to express sincere thanks to all those who have encouraged and helped me to write this book. My thanks are especially due to Professor John Rex (University of Warwick), Editor of the series of which this volume is part, Professor Sir Robert Birley (The City University, London), Professor Julius Gould (University of Nottingham), Mr Sonny Mehta (Executive Editor of Paladin Books), Mr Adrian Ziderman (Queen Mary College, University of London), Mr Michael Lyon (University of Aberdeen), and Mr A. Sivanandan, the Librarian of the Institute of Race Relations, London. I am also very grateful to my wife who has edited the manuscript. Finally, my thanks to Mrs Joyce Maxwell who typed the manuscript so expertly.

E.K.

1   Minorities and their Origins

Considerable attention has been focused of late on the coloured minority groups which have settled in Britain in the last fifteen years, and on the attitudes of the English population towards these groups. This interest is still heightening as special relationships develop between the newcomers and the English. It is my contention that a proper understanding of these relationships can be gained only by adopting a broader perspective – by comparing these groups with other minorities, that is European and older established groups. This comparative approach will inevitably be open to criticism. Each minority, it may be claimed, is distinctive in its background, its physical and cultural characteristics, and the historical context in which it settled in Britain. Yet, as will be amply illustrated, the similarities between their experiences are striking. A comparative study is certainly warranted, for it can not only uncover the common patterns which develop in societies experiencing inter-ethnic relations, but can also highlight and explain differences between each minority in its own particular relation to the majority, differences which may vitally matter.

It is in any event essential to understand the circumstances in which the various minorities have settled in this country as well as their backgrounds, and eventually to fill in some of the essential factual information about such aspects as their numbers and occupations. Our knowledge of how many coloured people there are in Britain today, or how many Cypriots or Jews live in London, may be wanting in accuracy, but our notions about the background of present-day immigrants or of the ancestors of other people who are not regarded as fully English although born here, are vaguer still. What sort of places have the Irish or the Poles come from – mostly villages? Where did the Jews live before they settled here? Why are Indians and Pakistanis so eager to gain a foothold in Britain? Have Jamaicans no other culture basically than that which British colonization offered to them when – through slavery – they lost their original way of life?

These background pictures of present-day minorities must first be drawn in before an intelligent appraisal of the contemporary position in Britain can be presented. The label 'minority' applies here broadly to all those groups which by virtue of ethnic differences – i.e. racial, religious, national, linguistic and other cultural factors – are singled out for differential treatment, and in consequence regard themselves as objects of collective discrimination. This follows the view of Louis Wirth who stresses that there is always a dominant group enjoying higher status alongside minority groups.[1] Minority status is not only lower; it means exclusion from full participation. It means, as Ruth Glass points out, a marginal location, a not-belonging or not-quite-belonging, being apart, being outsiders.[2] It is this qualitative aspect, rather than the quantitative factor of being fewer in number, that really matters.

Whilst I adopt a broad definition for 'ethnic minority' I fully recognize that some characteristics, such as the racial factor, may lead to special situations. Two Government White Papers in 1964 emphasized that in the case of Commonwealth immigrants 'the evidence laid more stress on the hostility towards [them] stemming directly from colour prejudice', and that to assume that the problem is temporary is to ignore 'the fact of physical differences which are visible and which will be handed on to the children'.[3] It is true of course that such race awareness may persist for several generations and may even perpetuate a 'colour line' in society, that is a social division based on colour. But such a situation is *socially* defined and not simply genetically determined. In this sense the coloured minorities are basically no different from the other minority groups whose situations are similarly the outcome of social attitudes, shaped as they may be by religious or national rather than racial criteria.

I shall now turn my attention to a discussion, in some

detail, of the various minorities, focusing on their countries of origin, the reasons why they left and their general cultural background.

The Cypriots

The island of Cyprus, a former colony of Britain from 1914,[4] lies in the Eastern Mediterranean and is a predominantly agricultural country. Its inhabitants have mostly been brought up in the six hundred or so villages widely scattered throughout the island. Many of the men will have worked for certain periods of time in the towns, but they retain their close ties with the villages where life centres around the institutions of church, school and coffee-house. The six district towns, including Nicosia the capital, are not highly industrialized and serve mainly as administrative and market centres. But this picture is changing rapidly as is seen most clearly in the substantial growth of the towns:

'Urbanization is only one of the many social changes which have come about on the island with the post-war programmes of economic development both before and after Independence in 1960. Emigration is, of course, another of these changes and is largely a reaction to the inability of the labour market to keep pace with the rising aspirations of a fast growing and youthful population'.[5]

There is another reason why many Cypriots have left their island: the Eoka troubles in the mid 1950s[6] and the strife between the Greek and Turkish communities were factors of a disruptive and depressing nature. The group solidarities of the once warring communities are still perpetuated in this country. The Greek Cypriots are Christians belonging to the Orthodox Church, while the Turkish Cypriots are Muslims. The religious, linguistic and other cultural differences between the two groups are most strongly reflected in that 'The emphasis is placed on the Greek-ness or Turkish-ness in their identity.'[7] The two groups constitute in reality two distinct ethnic minorities.

The Greek Cypriots, who are in the ratio of five to one Turkish Cypriot on the island, have managed to maintain their cultural values and way of life despite the 300 years of Turkish rule which preceded British rule until 1878. Their strong familial and kinship ties have played a major role in this. The British influence has also been slight and strongly resisted, as for instance in the educational field. This contrasts sharply with the West Indies where British culture struck roots easily. This is not surprising when we consider the strong cultural base that Greek Cypriots have inherited from the mainstream of Greek civilization; the Africans on the other hand were deprived of whatever culture they had when as slaves they were taken to the West Indies. But in spite of this the Greek Cypriots as well as the Turkish Cypriots who were given educational inducements under the Ottoman rule have emerged only slowly since the middle of this century from mass illiteracy. Illiteracy fell from 73 per cent in 1911 to 33 per cent in 1946, and to 18 per cent in 1960, the last figure being accounted for mainly by the elderly women in the population.[8]

The West Indians

These immigrants have come largely from a few of the very densely populated Caribbean islands. Sixty per cent are from Jamaica, taken over by the British in 1670 and which now has a population of nearly one and three quarter million. Jamaica has a population density of 374 per square mile, which is high compared say with India's 293 persons per square mile. The others come mainly from the smaller islands of Tobago, Trinidad and Barbados; from other islands dotted in a semi-circle on the Eastern Caribbean Sea, namely the Virgin Islands, Leeward Islands and Windward Islands; and from the Central American mainland areas of British Honduras and British Guiana. While the mainland territories are sparsely inhabited, some of the smaller islands have very high population densities. Barbados with its quarter of a million inhabitants has the phenomenal density of 1,380 persons per square mile, leaving well behind countries regarded as thickly populated, like Japan and Britain with densities of 583 and 536 respectively.[9]

The main reason for the West Indians emigrating is in

fact the pressure of population. The build-up in population was due primarily to the development of a lucrative sugar industry in the West Indies, operated, as elsewhere in the New World, by means of the plantation worked by cheap slave labour. This industry necessitated cheap labour on a large scale and the demand was met by the capture or purchase of millions of African slaves by merchant adventurers, who sold the slaves to the new colonies. Michael Banton writes that: 'England benefited greatly from the "triangular trade" whereby manufactured goods (rum, brandy, cloth, trinkets, iron bars and weapons) were sold in Africa, and slaves were bought for sale on the other side of the Atlantic, where sugar, tobacco, cotton and rum were to be purchased'.[10]

By 1834 this trading system took a quarter of a million slaves to Jamaica alone and tens of thousands more slaves to the other islands. The profitability of this kind of trading and of the plantation system is demonstrated by a number of facts. For instance, when in 1775 Jamaica imposed extra duty on imported slaves this was disallowed by the Board of Trade in London on the grounds that it 'could not allow the colonies to check or discourage in any degree a traffic so beneficial.[11] And when in 1807 the slave trade was abolished and in 1833 slaveholding in overseas British territories was forbidden, the planters in the West Indies started recruiting workers by means of the 'indenture' system (started in 1869) which meant free passage to and from the colony and a fixed wage for a definite number of years to be worked on the plantation. In this way Trinidad during the second half of the nineteenth century and up to the First World War attracted some 150,000 workers mainly from India and China.[12] This kind of influx as well as the settlement of small numbers of Europeans has created a mixed race which is now labelled as West Indian.

By the twentieth century the exploitation of economic advantages from these colonies passed its peak and the whole region became troubled by an unstable economy, the main reason for which was too great a reliance on one major product: sugar. There was also a lack of capital investment for modernization. The population of the West Indies therefore began to look to other countries for employment in order to escape widespread poverty. They emigrated in the early years of this century to Cuba to work on the sugar estates there, and to Panama to work on the canal. Subsequently, they turned in ever-increasing numbers to the United States itself,[13] but in 1952 the passing of the McCarran Act closed this door to them. Only small numbers of West Indians came to Britain before that date, mainly through the recruitment of West Indian servicemen during the Second World War.[14] It is since the early 1950s that the large influx has been experienced in Britain, a direct consequence, it would appear, of the McCarran Act.

The fate that befell the Negro slave in the West Indies was not very different from that of his brethren in the States, so clearly described by Franklin Frazier.[15] Once in a slave coffle they were made into 'animate tools' to be used in the abject misery of the plantation system. Their former familial and cultural bonds having been ruthlessly destroyed they produced a simple folk society with the matriarchate at its centre. This was a necessity born out of circumstances. Slaves were encouraged to have children, for this was economically advantageous to the owners, but they were not allowed to marry. The selling of slaves[16] by one owner to another made a stable family life impossible. As a result some paternal roles were taken over by the owners, many of whom were the fathers of some of the children born to slave women. In such conditions the only stability was to be found in the relationship between a mother and her young children, a relationship that had a chance to persist through grown-up daughters and their children in turn.

As the West Indian population became emancipated and increasingly Christianized during the last century, the goal for the majority became the European pattern of family life. This was, however, unattainable for most of the working-class men until fairly late in life. The economically depressed West Indian's substitute was faithful concubinage, and he came to regard the marriage ceremony and home ownership as status symbols. As a result, traces of slavery are still visible in the family life of West Indians. The rate of illegitimacy in Jamaica, for instance, is 70 per cent and this is accepted as a normal phenomenon. But those who came to Britain have definitely moved in the direction of replacing the extended matriarchal family with a nuclear type of family grouping. This is giving rise in Britain to many problems and sometimes tragic circumstances. The relative deprived of the extended group may be left out on a limb, or the child of an immigrant father may be brought over to join a new family as a result of his father's marrying another girl in Britain. A new country, a new type of family, and a new educational system are often what the West Indian child has to contend with in Britain. As Katrin FitzHerbert says, 'he obviously has to make a superhuman adjustment', and 'many of the behavioural problems English schoolteachers encounter . . . result from this aspect of the migration'.[17]

There are a number of factors which suggest that West Indians have been strongly anglicized even before their arrival in this country. English, spoken with a particular dialect, is the mother tongue of most of them; they are familiar with English place-names and customs and with *the* English sport – cricket; most of them are Christian; and their educational system follows that of England. These points are undoubtedly true but one can go too far in claiming anglicization for the West Indian immigrants.[18] Most of them are drawn from the semi-rural colonial proletariat and the background of slavery has left a distinctive mark on their way of life, as for instance in regard to family organization.

In the sphere of religion although the Jamaican Census returns, for instance, showed that fifty-four per cent of the population belonged to the Anglican and Baptist Churches, most Jamaicans were not in fact firmly attached to these religions. In Jamaica, Christian sects and various quasi-Christian and non-Christian cults were the popular attractions. The immigrants in Britain have similarly shied away from established Churches and have opted for their own brand of Christian religion, particularly the Pentecostal sects.[19]

And as far as education is concerned, in Jamaica this did take on the English pattern, but only in the less important sense of following similar if outdated school curricula, examination systems and so on. Pedagogically the methods are Victorian, school attendance is not obligatory and is most irregular and the physical conditions in schools are generally of a very low standard.[20] It is not surprising, therefore, that in the 1950s the illiteracy rate in Jamaica was still nearly twenty per cent.[21] Illiteracy tends to be less prevalent in the younger, more go-ahead generation who on the whole make up the immigrants in Britain.

African Negroes

While this group contributes a rather small minority in Britain when compared with some of the much larger immigrant communities, the singling out of this group does serve to draw attention to the distinctness of the various groups which are often loosely called 'coloured'. The distinctness may manifest itself in the history of settlement in Britain and in social and cultural backgrounds as well as in genetic charac-teristics.

As we have seen, the West Indians are racially mixed, al-though they have a strong Negro base. It has been claimed that only 17 per cent of Jamaicans and 16 per cent of Trini-dadians are of mixed race but it is quite likely that these figures are unreliable. The racial composition of West Indians is extremely complex and contains all kinds of mixtures.[22] As against this there is obviously a far greater racial purity among African Negroes. Another difference is that although many of the African Negroes have been converted to Christianity and have been influenced by British colonial rule, on the whole they have retained their own tribal culture and language. Michael Banton notes that even among smaller groups of African Negroes with a common background and language, tribal societies and tribal solidarity linger on.[23] On the other hand as Judith Henderson says, the kind of unit based on a common past is not matched by the West Indians in Britain[24] presumably because they have lost their earlier cultural ante-cedence.

African Negroes, particularly from West Africa, are among the oldest established minority groups in Britain. It is re-corded that there were small numbers in this country even before 1600.[25] In the seventeenth and eighteenth centuries fashionable ladies liked to have Negro attendants, but there were still very few until the end of the eighteenth century. By the nineteenth century somewhat larger numbers came to England. There were two categories then: the seamen who came with other African and Asiatic seamen, such as Arabs from Aden, Somalis, Indians and Chinese, many of whom settled here in dockland areas; and the sons of chiefs and other notables who came to be educated in England.[26] The latter were the precursors of the large number of African and other coloured students in Britain today. The Negro seamen were joined by other contingents brought over in the First World War to work in munition factories and labour battalions, and these groups form the Negro working class in this country. The ranks of the Negro middle class here have been swollen mainly by students and other professional and business people encouraged by British missionaries and British business interests to seek training in this country.[27] Some of these British-trained people decided subsequently to stay on or return to this country.

Indians and Pakistanis

The Indian sub-continent is a vast area comparable in size to the whole of Europe excluding the Soviet Union. It has a teeming population of 550 million, India alone accounting for 450 million and Pakistan for 100 million. The two sovereign states are the result of the granting of independence and partition by Britain in 1947 for what was its most formidable dependency. The partition in 1947 was based on the predominance of the Hindu and Muslim religions in certain areas, but it could not avoid the continuation of enmity between the two groups represented by the new states, as evidenced particularly in the unresolved dispute over the province of Kashmir.

Although there has been a tradition of emigration from the two north-westerly states of Punjab and Gujurat, because of the pressure on land and widespread unemployment,[28] the partition had the effect of enhancing migration from these two regions. In both cases the regions have become border areas between India and West Pakistan, as did Kashmir, a factor which has unsettled millions of people and has given rise to increased migration since partition. It is true that – as most writers stress – the main inducement for migration has been the phenomenally high incomes it is possible to achieve in Britain as compared with incomes in India and Pakistan. It is also true that Indian seamen, mainly from the maritime areas of present-day East Pakistan (divided by nearly a thousand miles from West Pakistan), settled in small numbers in British dockland areas, together with other Asians and Africans, throughout the last century, and that, like the African Negroes, Indians have had their middle class of students and businessmen here for a long time. The large numbers, however, have come since partition and to these have been added, particularly since 1967, sizeable groups of Indians who have had to leave East Africa, their first area of settlement, as a consequence of the Africanization programmes[29] in such countries as Kenya and Tanzania.

The population of India and Pakistan is racially varied and contains, mainly in complex admixtures, all the racial elements of mankind. It contains Negroid as well as Caucasoid elements, which bring it into close genetic relationship with Europeans. The social structure of India is characterized by village, kin and caste. Being a predominantly agricultural country the village community with its close unity and control is the mainstay of society. Industrialization, particularly in the last two decades, has made important strides and urbanization is evident in the existence and growth of large inland cities and ports. The industrial-urban sector of the economy, however, is still very much of secondary importance quantitatively although it is making certain inroads on the quality of life not only in town but indirectly in the Indian village too. Nevertheless, the kinship system of the Indians continues to be one which was extremely well suited to the form of traditional agriculture pursued. This system is the patriarchal extended family, which can be defined as '*all* the living members of a family of all generations in the male line, who live communally and share everything'.[30] In this extended kin group the male head has strong controlling power. In addition the individual is controlled by the *jati* to which he belongs. This is a sub-caste or caste-like unit which, as Zinkin says, 'gives Hindu society its character, its typical fragmentation into small groups within which people live and outside which they, and particularly the women, keep their contacts to minimum'.[31] The Hindu's *jati* is part of a wider religious-caste system, as his village is part of a larger linguistic area. He is at the centre of a number of concentric circles, and it is the extended family, the *jati* and the village, the circles closest around him, which influence him most. This pattern reverberates in the life of the Indian when he becomes an immigrant. It will be found that the Indian in Britain has come here through the sponsorship of a member of his village-kin group. He continues his close association with this group, as evidenced by continuous contact with his original folk in India, by his reliance for help and friendship on other members of his group in this country, and by the reciprocation of such help.[32]

Eighty-five per cent of Indians are Hindu by religion. This religion is basically monotheistic in that it stresses belief in one god, but it contains elements of polytheism, which is not surprising considering that it grew out of the mingling of the religions of Aryan invaders and the peoples they conquered some thousands of years ago. The Hindu religion sanctions the caste system, which is a rigid stratification of society in terms of strict occupational divisions and social exclusiveness. The religious sanctioning consists in a belief that however lowly placed an individual, good conduct is rewarded by his ascent on the social ladder to a higher caste in a later life, an ascent achieved by the reincarnation of his soul.[33] An important reform movement, although adhered to by only 2.3 per cent of the population, was that of the Sikh religion. This stresses the importance of monotheism, ousting the polytheistic tendencies of Hinduism, and it proclaims the brotherhood of all men, thus rejecting the caste system. The Sikhs in Britain are far out of proportion in relation to other Indians compared to their numerical strength in India. They are discernible by their turbans and other traditional garb; many, particularly of the older generation, never cut their hair; and all are supposed to be teetotallers and non-smokers.

The Pakistanis differ of course in that they have the Muslim religion and are unaffected by the caste system which, incidentally, is now becoming weaker even in Hindu society. But in many other respects the Pakistani's background is not all that different from that of the Indian. He, too, is normally a villager and subject to the close ties of the extended family. The languages spoken are in some cases shared by Indians and Pakistanis, particularly when they come from areas bordering on each other, as for instance around Punjab. In other cases an East Pakistani who speaks Bengali may not be able to communicate with a West Pakistani who speaks Punjabi. Similarly Indians from the North who speak one of the Hindu-Urdu group of languages which come from the same stock as most European languages may not be able to converse with Indians from the South who speak pre-Aryan Dravidian tongues.[34]

Although the Indo-Pakistani culture has an illustrious past, modern educational standards are extremely low. Only 15 per cent of the population of Pakistan is literate, and only about one third of the Indians are estimated to be literate. But most of the Indians in Britain come from the Punjab and Gujarat areas in which there is a very much higher literacy rate in their own languages. Again most Indians have a good working knowledge of English. On the whole Pakistanis have lower literacy rates and generally cannot speak English.[35]

The Chinese

The East India Company introduced the earliest Chinese settlers to this country. They were usually employed as seamen by the company but a very small minority were left on shore. There was official reference to these Chinese seamen as early as 1814, but throughout the nineteenth century their numbers remained very small. Up to the first part of this century, Chinese seamen continued to settle here and we may refer to these settlers as the older immigrants, originating mainly from the Kwantung province of China and from Hong Kong. The provinces of Kwantung and Fukien in South China were traditional emigration areas. Their fast growing populations, consisting mainly of poor peasants and artisans, have usually sought to improve their lot by settling in South-East Asia, Australia, New Zealand and America, with only a handful reaching the shores of Britain.

Since the Second World War a more substantial stream of immigrants has reached Britain. This newer category is a mixed group with regard to country or area of origin and occupation. It includes Malaysian Chinese as well as Chinese from Hong Kong and the New Territories and occupationally it ranges from businessmen and restaurant workers to nurses and students. As Ng Kwee Choo says these newer immigrants 'have little in common except that they are Chinese by "race" and speak the English language, for in this group several different dialects are spoken and its members originate from different countries'.[36] These newer immigrants are more highly educated than the members of the older group.

The newer group of Chinese immigrants, despite its heterogeneity, has a strong link with Hong Kong as the largest number originate from there. Hong Kong became a colony in 1843 and its territory was enlarged in 1860 and again in 1898 when the Kowloon Peninsula and Stonecutters Island and additional lands around it were incorporated. Competition against Portuguese traders and an attempt to break down Chinese restrictionism led eventually to the acquisition by war of this colony which in 1841 was 'a barren island with hardly a house upon it'.[37] By the middle of the twentieth century this had been transformed into a modern city and a highly overpopulated Western outpost on the fringes of Communist China. Although light industry is highly developed in Hong Kong City many of the inhabitants of the colony are engaged in fishing and farming. The economic opportunities for the population of over three million have been insufficient, however, and this is the main factor that has led to emigration. An investigation into the causes of emigration among a sample of Southern Chinese has shown that the two principal factors are economic pressure and previous connexion with other parts of South-East Asia, such as Malaysia.[38]

Although we distinguished between earlier immigrants and the more heterogeneous group from Hong Kong and

Malaysia who have come over since the Second World War, the members of both categories are mainly from South China and mostly belong to the Cantonese and Hakka dialect groups. So far as religion is concerned, this is not as widespread or well organized as in most of the other minority groups, but when a Chinese does identify with a religion it is, as a rule, with Buddhism.[39]

The Irish

An exchange of population between two sister islands is a natural phenomenon and it is one that applied to England and Ireland early in their recorded histories. It is known that there were small Irish settlements, particularly of merchants, in some English cities early in the twelfth century, and that by the year 1400 there were substantial Irish colonies mainly in the ports, that is in London, Liverpool and Bristol.[40]

The relationship between Ireland and England has not been a happy one particularly from the time of Cromwell's war in 1649. Since the Reformation in the sixteenth century there has also been religious schism between Protestant England and Catholic Ireland. Taking the island as a whole, 75 per cent of its population is Catholic. A feeling of bitterness towards England continued right up to the disturbances before the creation of the Irish Free State in 1921 and has not yet disappeared. Despite the geographical proximity of Ireland to Great Britain and in a broad sense the sharing of common historical circumstances, these differences have persisted. The fact that the Irish, unlike the English, are Celts[41] may have something to do with this. On the other hand the Irish did not have better treatment at the hands of the Scottish Celts[42] with whom they share not only a basically common stock but also the Gaelic tongue and other cultural features. A good deal of the resentment of the Irish by the Scots and the English stemmed from religious differences and much of the Irish bitterness regarding the English concerned the latter's domination.

English domination was the principal factor which led to

migration. The economic dimension of the domination is clearly described by J. A. Jackson:

From the beginning of the eighteenth century living standards were steadily reduced by the high rents demanded by absentee landlords (mainly English) for sub-divided and often unproductive land. Mercantilist economic policy in England prevented Ireland from exporting livestock, woollen manufacture was suppressed and industry and trade were threatened with collapse. Widespread poverty and indolence were the result of a long-continued policy of suppression and denial towards Ireland in economic affairs, politics, education and religion.[43]

In the second half of the century trade between Ireland and England improved, but Ireland could not compete with the latter due to poor natural resources and lack of capital investment. Its industry, without local coal or iron, was therefore slow to develop, whilst its agriculture took the wrong course. The increase in cattle trading in the latter part of the century turned much of Irish land to pasturage and this led to an ever-increasing dependence on the potato as a staple food for the increasing population. Despite crop failures and consequent famines during the eighteenth century, such as in 1741, no important changes towards crop diversification were made and Ireland plunged into the disastrous mid-nineteenth century when its population was decimated by one million people due to the great famine of 1846 and 1847.

It was this economic inability of Ireland to support its growing population, coupled with a wish to escape domination, not least in the religious sphere, which prompted the large-scale exodus from Ireland. The vast population movement was at first directed primarily to the United States where opportunities for improvement were greatest. After the great famine years one million emigrated to that country alone.[44] To a lesser extent immigrants sought their new homes in Canada, Australia and New Zealand as well as in Britain. But it was principally after the imposition of strict Irish quotas by the United States, between 1920 and 1929, that Britain became the main recipient of Irish immigrants.

The two main categories among the Irish are the Dubliners

and other townspeople, and the 'culchies' or countrymen who predominate in numbers.[45] Their family background is patriarchal[46] with a strong concern for unity, security and a good reputation. The unity is reflected in the bonds maintained between people who have emigrated and the original families back home. Security is seen as demanding that to be eligible to marry a young girl must have a dowry, whilst a young man must have the ability to keep a family. It has been difficult for these requirements to be met. The tradition of the older generation holding on to the family farm and the generally depressed economic conditions have been unfavourable for the attainment of these ideals for large numbers. Hence the high proportion of unmarried men and women among the Irish and the very high percentage of illegitimate births.[47] One way out of such situations is emigration, which has in fact become an absolutely natural process to the Irish. Whilst stressing the institutionalization of migration it should be noted that not all this movement in population carries a character of permanency in settlement. There is a good deal of to and fro in these population shifts, evidenced by the nineteenth-century harvesters and the twentieth-century building workers. This has been facilitated by the greater proximity and the familiarity with England that applies to the Irish much more than to the other minority groups.

The Jews

The very long history of the Jews in their role as the minority *par excellence* and their variegated experience in moving from one country to another, almost relentlessly, is reflected quite clearly in their relationship with England.

The earliest Jews to arrive in this country were probably among travellers who sought out the fringes of the expanded Roman Empire, some time during the first millennium of the Christian era. A Jewish community was well established in Norman England. This was a direct outcome of the expansion of the English economy and its greater integration into continental Europe, processes in which Jewish merchants played an important role. The kings of England were also accustomed to use Jewish financiers, particularly in times of trouble. This was a serious weakness for the community, for it meant that as the royal appetite grew the Jewish money dealer was forced to be more exacting in his demands to borrowers. Hence the hostility of the population, leading to violence against them and their impoverishment in the thirteenth century, after about one century of prosperity. The kings abandoned them and under the pretext of respect for the Church Edward I ordered their expulsion in 1290.[48]

Some Jewish Marranos lived in London during the sixteenth century after their expulsion from Spain in 1492. The Marranos lived officially as Christians but often practised Judaism secretly. In 1656 Cromwell readmitted Jews to England and the first batch consisted of Sephardi Jews, that is, those who originated from Spain and Portugal but were now living in other parts of Western Europe, particularly in Holland.[49] During the eighteenth and the early part of the nineteenth century these Jews were joined by small numbers of their Ashkenazi brethren, that is Jews who did not follow the route through North Africa to the Iberian Peninsula but settled after the Roman conquest of Palestine on the European continent, mainly in German lands. Most of the Jews from Western Europe, whether Sephardi or Ashkenazi, were townspeople and, in the main, merchants. A totally different stream of migrants overtook this earlier settlement towards the end of the nineteenth century. These were East European Jews who were fleeing in large numbers from the poverty-stricken areas of Russia, Poland and Rumania, and escaping the terror and pogroms by Tsarist Russia. These were Ashkenazi Jews who had settled in the rural areas of Eastern Europe and were either farmers or small artisans emanating from the lesser towns of the region.[50] These Jews, unlike the earlier settlers in England, had a strong working-class background.[51]

The largest waves of Jewish immigrants came after the worst Russian pogroms of 1881. Very often the immigrants, whose aim was to reach the United States via Britain, remained in this country, unable to complete their journey for lack of funds. The usual route was by sea from a port in the Baltic to Hull; and from there across England to Liverpool, from where the sea journey could be continued to America. Many, however, settled in the above-mentioned ports or the intermediate large industrialized towns such as Leeds and Manchester.[52] London was itself a receiving port and had of course its own magnetism.

The East European Jewish immigration had come to an almost complete halt by the time of the First World War. But in the 1930s another, smaller, wave of Jewish refugees arrived in England: those persecuted in Nazi Germany and other occupied lands. These formed the last substantial Jewish group to settle in this country. They were mainly middle-class people with a high percentage of professionals in the fields of science, medicine and the arts.

It is clear that the socio-economic background of the Jews in Britain is a complex one and that their length of settlement varies according to the immigration waves that brought them here. Even though they are all adherents of the Jewish religion, there is heterogeneity also in their religious and cultural backgrounds. Most of those who came from Western Europe tended to practise Judaism in a less overt fashion and were regarded by the late arrivals from Eastern Europe as 'reformed'. The East Europeans claimed to be the bearers of the authentic religious values and their organizations have been labelled as 'orthodox'. For all Jews, however, the central binding force was the synagogue and the immigrants perpetuated this in their new surroundings. Culturally the unifying element has been the study of the Talmud, the lengthy commentaries on the written and oral laws of the Old Testament. The stress in Judaism on the study of these commentaries for their own sake and inherent value has produced an exceptionally favourable orientation towards learning *per se* among Jews. The educative function of all institutions has been harnessed, therefore, in the Jewish minority. The family itself, nuclear in type but encouraging kin ties, was regarded as a microcosmic competing ground within which erudition and achievement could be exhibited. Success in business was often taken to reflect shrewd intelligence. And the synagogue and other religious institutions were ideally, and often in practice, mainly houses of learning. Illiteracy was, in fact, almost unknown even among East European Jews. The original Hebrew was maintained mainly by the Rabbis, but became restricted among the majority of Jews for use as a language for prayer. Among Western immigrants the vernacular was usually that of the country of birth, whilst among East Europeans Yiddish, a jargon of German and Hebrew with some Slavonic influence, became accepted. In fact a rich Yiddish culture and folk-lore, steeped in Judaic values but with a strong East European flavour, flourished particularly during the late nineteenth and early twentieth century.[53]

Poles and other East Europeans

Poland, one of the larger East European countries outside the Soviet Union has not had a long history of emigration. There had been a certain amount of population outflow from Polish territories since the Napoleonic Wars in the late eighteenth century. Emigration on a smaller scale was maintained, through most of the nineteenth century, by a wish to escape foreign rule. Towards the twentieth century, however, a larger migration, induced by the search for better economic opportunities and directed mainly towards the United States, overtook Poland as it did most other European countries. Small numbers at the turn of the century came to Britain too, but most of those described as Poles, as in the case of Russians, were in fact Jews emanating from these countries.

The substantial settlement of Polish Christians in Britain came with certain events connected with the Second World War. To begin with, a Polish Government-in-exile fled early on in the war to Britain. It was bitterly disappointed by the Yalta agreement between the Allies which incorporated East Poland into the USSR. Consequently the British Government felt, it seems, that it had to assume greater responsibility towards the Poles and its opportunity to do so came at the end of the war. In December 1945 there were nearly a quarter of a million soldiers in the Polish Forces under British Command.[54] The largest number belonged to the Second Polish Corps who fought with the Allies under General Wladyslaw Anders. This was composed mainly of Poles who had been deported

27

to Russia in 1939–40 but who later were allowed to join Anders's forces. When the war ended the alternatives of repatriation to Poland, emigration to other countries, or establishment in Britain were open. The Government encouraged this last by forming a Polish Resettlement Corps in 1947 which was joined by 114,000 Poles who opted to stay in Britain as civilians. More than 100,000, mainly peasants, returned to Poland and many emigrated to such countries as Brazil and Canada. Those who stayed were joined by their dependants,[55] so that within a few years a strong Polish community was established in this country.

Most of the Poles who settled here did so for a political reason: unwillingness to live in a Communist country dominated by Russia. It was perhaps Polish nationalism and enmity towards Russia more than the political system adopted in Poland which motivated most of the Poles.

A similar feeling of distrust and antagonism to Russian domination led to emigration from other East European countries. At the time of the Hungarian uprising in 1956, and again after the Russian invasion of Czechoslovakia in 1968, small groups of political refugees came to settle in Britain. Earlier on in the post-war period, however, other groups of East Europeans and those from Baltic nations came to Britain in quite different circumstances. In 1946 there were about one million Displaced Persons in camps in Europe. The British Government decided to tap this manpower so as to recharge its labour force, depleted by the ravages of war, a step which appeared necessary in order to carry out the task of rebuilding the country and its economy.[56] In 1947, therefore, the Ministry of Labour started to recruit in the camps what it termed European Voluntary Workers, mostly Ukrainians, Poles, Latvians, Lithuanians and others from the Baltic and East European regions. Within a short period more than 90,000 of these workers settled in Britain.[57]

The East Europeans, excluding the Jews, are of course Christians, and due to the predominance of the Poles amongst those who settled here, the Catholic Church gained most from this influx. Although most of the East Europeans come from rural backgrounds, in the sense that their countries were at the time of their departure mainly agricultural, many of those who settled here were skilled workers, and not a few were professional people. This was due to the fact that amongst the Poles, as mentioned above, a self-selection process took place whereby most of the peasants from the armed forces returned to their ancestral lands in Poland; and also to the fact that among the EVWs the Ministry of Labour sought the more skilled people, and that among the 'new' East Europeans, that is Hungarians and Czechs, the younger, better educated people, particularly students, were those more willing to move at times of crisis and ready to seek out Britain and other Western countries.

Concluding comments

The minority groups whose backgrounds I have covered do not account for all the immigrants or refugees who sought new homes in Britain. The Jews were not the only ones to be persecuted for their religion or ethnic separateness. The Calvinist French Huguenots, who were not tolerated by their Catholic brethren, came in fair numbers after the horrible massacre of St Bartholomew's Day in 1572, but the bulk arrived only after the revocation of the Edict of Nantes in 1685. Similarly small numbers of Armenians fled due to the Turkish massacres after 1894. In recent times migrants seeking more favourable economic opportunities in this country have come not only from the West Indies and Cyprus but also from Italy, Spain and Malta. However the groups described do cover all the largest minorities, as well as a few smaller communities.

More generally all these groups have to be considered (a) in terms of the reasons in the original country and the receiving country which were directly conducive to immigration; and (b) in terms of the processes involved in migration. Regarding the first point it is true that in the case of many minorities some particular 'push' factor is discernible as playing a leading role in influencing people to move. The Poles and Hungarians in Britain are primarily political refugees. The underlying reason for the Irish and most of the coloured immigration is economic – often simply the quest for work. The Jews, particularly if one considers different waves of immigrants, were influenced by a multiplicity of 'push' factors: religious persecution, political inequality and lack of economic opportunities. Looking now at the 'pull' factors again we see that in some cases humanitarianism was primarily responsible for allowing immigrants into Britain, examples being given by the Huguenots and Jews. In other cases the economic self-interest of Britain, the receiving country, induced the influx, as in the case of the recruitment of the European Voluntary Workers to solve the post-war manpower problem in such industries as mining, agriculture, building and textiles,[58] or in the case of West Indians, Indians and Pakistanis to help man the transport and other public services. And yet in another way the latter groups instanced had an advantageous position also because of the historical links they had with the receiving country: they were within the framework of the Empire and the Commonwealth. In the case of the Irish, J. A. Jackson argues in fact that:

One must look for causes as a complex pattern of influences at many levels which, in Ireland, arise from a particular set of circumstances which have a bearing on the individual's decision to emigrate. This pattern links economic, demographic, historical and social causes; factors of 'pull' and of 'push' resulting in a social fabric which produces, and is sustained by, emigration.[59]

To put it in a nutshell, the young Irishman of a large poverty-stricken traditional rural family living in a country with a stagnating economy will easily be attracted to a well remunerated unskilled job in the expanding building industry of some large urban centre in a much more prosperous economy and freer society obtaining in not very distant Great Britain.

Ceri Peach stresses the need to see Britain in a larger geographical-economic context in which the close inter-relationship between 'push' and 'pull' factors comes clearly to the fore. He cites some figures about migration to other West European countries. In 1963 West Germany had 804,000 foreign workers mostly from Southern Europe but including 34,000 Afro-Asians. This was in addition to the thirteen million East Germans who had settled in West Germany since the war. By the end of 1964 France received 520,000 Algerian Muslims in addition to other groups. The Algerians alone formed a larger group than our West Indian, Indian and Pakistani immigrants at the time.[60] The Netherlands similarly experienced an influx of immigrants. Nearly 300,000 Indonesians settled there between 1945 and 1959. In addition the Netherlands had in 1968 about 80,000 workers from various countries of Europe and particularly from Turkey and Morocco, as well as smaller numbers from Surinam and the Antilles.[61] In all these cases political factors played an unmistakable role in allowing the population shifts. West Germany's assumption of responsibility for Germans from the East and its closer links with Italy through the Common Market is a clear example. France's links with its former Algerian dependency, Netherland's link with Indonesia and the similar position of Britain and its former colonies are further examples. But it can be argued that the political links mask the all-important economic factors, and also that mistakenly the 'push' factor in sending countries has been overemphasized, thus neglecting the dynamic attraction of receiving countries. The significant fact is the new industrial expansion in North-West Europe at a pace which left the gap between this part of the world and other less developed areas, whether in Southern Europe or in tropical regions in Africa, Asia and the Caribbean, even wider than before. It is not that poverty is new in Southern Europe or that poverty in the West Indies was not influencing its people to migrate, but that 'industrial prosperity, on its present scale, is new in northern Europe'. This development has increased the demand for unskilled as well as skilled labour and it has naturally brought about 'a radical extension of the areas that supply this need.'[62]

However, with the extension of the area has come also an increase in the volume of migration. It is this increase which has figured, rightly or wrongly, as one of the main bones of contention in discussions of immigration, a matter dealt with below. The actual process involved in the increase of immigration is most frequently that known as 'chain migration'. Charles Price has studied this phenomenon in Australia in some detail and has shown for example how it applied in particular to non-British immigrants.[63] A few immigrants, once settled in the receiving country, send for their close dependants, other relatives and friends. As Anthony Richmond puts it: 'Once migration has started on a small scale the process tends to become cumulative. Knowledge of the attractive features of the new land is conveyed from relative to relative and from friend to friend. Letters written home by the early migrants when they have succeeded in obtaining remunerative employment encourage others to follow'.[64] In this way whole groups, sometimes numbering hundreds, from the same original location tend to be transplanted to a relatively confined area in the new country. This was very much the case with East European Jews who came to Britain.[65] For the Irish J. A. Jackson shows how typically many families have been depleted of the majority of their members through migration to England.[66] As for West Indians it has been claimed that some areas of particular islands predominate in certain districts or even streets in London.[67] The effect of this process on the 'ghettoization' of the immigrants is another point I shall discuss later. First, however, we turn in the next chapter to a consideration of the facts regarding the geographical location of the minority groups, their numerical strength and other basic descriptive data.

2   Basic Statistics

A basic requirement for an account of minority groups in this country is to furnish reliable statistical information regarding the size and other demographic characteristics of these groups, their geographical location, housing and occupational distribution. I propose to deal here only with the demography and location of these minorities, leaving housing and occupation for Chapter 4.

There are no comprehensive official statistics about minorities for historical reasons and also because certain democratic principles are said to be in danger if officialdom is allowed to question citizens of this country about their colour, religion or national origin. The Census does, however, ask for place of birth and this is of some value in arriving at total estimates. In 1971 the Census will also ask questions about the year of first entry into this country of those born overseas and the country of birth of respondents and their parents. Information thus gained will greatly improve our statistics about minorities. But the returns of previous Censuses do not contain data necessary for accurately distinguishing ethnic minorities from the rest of the population.

Certain Government departments, such as the Home Office and the Ministry of Labour, and local authorities, particularly their education and housing departments, do have some figures. The Immigration Authorities, for instance, have kept some records about the number of Commonwealth immigrants who have come into the country, but these go back only to 1955. Local education authorities often do have fairly accurate estimates of children in their schools belonging to different national, religious, racial and linguistic groups. Examples of such information could be multiplied, but the essential point

33

is that altogether they do not easily add up to a clear, comprehensive and reliable sociography of Britain's minority populations.

The picture becomes even more blurred if we go back a century. The influence of *laissez-faire* meant that Britain had no passport system and until the Aliens Act of 1905 Jews from Eastern Europe, for instance, could enter the country freely. Again, for historical reasons population movement between the United Kingdom and Ireland has always been free. It is impossible therefore to say with any exactitude how many Irish people have settled in England or how many Jews came here in the years before the twentieth century.

In addition we have to contend with a number of complicating factors. Lack of official statistics means that the natural increase of minority populations is not accurately known. Re-emigration, particularly prevalent among Poles, Jews and East Europeans, many of whom were able to proceed to the 'New World' after a shorter sojourn in Britain, is another factor to be taken into account. And finally there is the process of assimilation through which minorities do become numerically diminished. By the intermarriage of coloured and white people and the eventual ability of the subsequently mixed generations to 'pass' into the general population; the religious conversion for instance of some Jews; or by complete changes in the cultural and political outlook of Poles or Irish and the concomitant shift in their identification from the minority to the majority, ethnic groups are altered and anyone undertaking to produce estimates of their size or project their future must of necessity take such factors into consideration.

Despite these difficulties there has been sufficient research in this field to enable us to present reliable estimates of the larger minority groups.

Numbers

The largest single minority group is the Irish. The 1966 Census shows that there were 698,000 Irish immigrants in England and Wales. The figure does not include those from Northern Ireland. In 1961 an estimate of Irish-born residing in Britain, including both British citizens from Northern Ireland and citizens of the Irish Republic, was given as 870,000. Another estimate for the same year put the Irish-born at over one million.[1] It is of course difficult to say how many of the Irish-born were members of families which included others born in this country but who obviously were part of the Irish community.

The Jews follow next with a total of 410,000 estimated for 1965.[2] The largest coloured minority is the Jamaican numbering 273,800 in 1966.[3] Of course if one lumps together all the coloured minorities the estimate for these given for 1968 is 1,113,000.[4] But this includes diverse groups which must be regarded as distinct minorities, such as the 223,000 Indians, the 119,000 Pakistanis, and the 60,000 people from the Far East and the 50,000 from West Africa. Other sizeable minority groups are the Poles who number about 130,000[5] and the Cypriots about 100,000.[6]

Then come the smaller groups for some of which there are no reliable estimates. It is known for instance that over 90,000 European Voluntary Workers settled here shortly after the Second World War,[7] but this figure included Ukrainians, Latvians, Lithuanians, Estonians, Hungarians, Czechs and other nationalities. Between 1956 and 1957 nearly 15,000[8] more Hungarians settled in this country and in 1968 tiny numbers of Czechs were allowed to settle here. The estimates for these smaller minorities are difficult to obtain. At the same time it should be noted that there are largish groups of Americans (87,000), Australians (62,000) and various West European nationalities such as Italians (96,000) living in Britain. The 1966 Census found that altogether there were 837,000 foreign immigrants living in England and Wales, whilst the number born overseas including those from Commonwealth countries and Eire was 2,478,000.[9] Figures concerning those born overseas are not very useful, however. For whilst Australians enter into calculations many Jews do not, since they are British-born. Yet Australians do not form a minority community in the sense in which we use that term[10] any more than Scotsmen do, whilst Jews can definitely be distinguished as such a community.

It is well-nigh impossible, in the present state of knowledge, to give a complete numerical account of all the minority groups in this country. What we do, however, in Table 2.1 is to give comparative figures and the percentages that they make up of the total population, for a number of larger minority groups about which sufficient information exists. The total population figure used is that given by the 1966 Census for England and Wales, that is 47 million.

TABLE 2.1: *Size and Percentage of the Larger Minority Groups*

Minority group	Size	Per cent of total population
Irish	2,000,000*	4·2
West Indian	454,000	1·0
Jewish	410,000	0·9
Indian & Pakistani	359,000	0·8
Polish	130,000	0·3
Cypriot	100,000	0·2

* This figure must be treated as a very general estimate in the absence of any reliable statistical data.[11]

The figure for the Irish is a general estimate. The 1966 Census, through questions on place of birth, traced nearly 700,000 Irish immigrants. There are also their British-born offspring. In addition the Irish community may claim some of the descendants of earlier generations of immigrants. These sources taken together are estimated to form an Irish community of approximately two million, and without any doubt, and whatever the accurate figure may be, they constitute the largest single minority group.

Taking all coloured groups together, they represent only 2·4 per cent of the entire population. The West Indians on their own, for instance, make up barely 1 per cent whilst the Jews fall short even of this tiny proportion. Adding together all distinguishable minority and immigrant groups, however, we find that they reach somewhere around four and a quarter million, or 9 per cent of the total population. The figure of 9 per cent includes, of course, people from all over the world; the coloured groups make up less than a third of this overall figure.

Irish immigration has been maintained at a very high level over a very long period. There were over 600,000 Irish-born persons in England and Wales in 1861 and, as we have seen above, just over a hundred years later the number of Irish-born was considerably higher. Figures for Irish-born shown by Censuses over the last century and a quarter have always been well above a quarter of a million and usually nearer the half-million mark.[12] The heaviest periods of Jewish immigration were from 1881 to 1914, when the Jewish population rose from 65,000 to over a quarter of a million, and 1933 to 1940 when some 73,000 Jewish refugees came to Britain but of whom, it has been estimated, only about 40,000 settled here.[13] The Poles and other East Europeans, excluding Jews, came mainly after the Second World War. In 1947 114,000 joined the Polish Resettlement Corps, thus opting to stay permanently in Britain, and this group had another 33,000 dependants brought over. In the last years of the 1940s mainly East European workers were being recruited by the Ministry of Labour from Displaced Persons' camps, of whom

FIGURE 1: *Population Growth of Immigrants in England and Wales from Selected Commonwealth Countries**

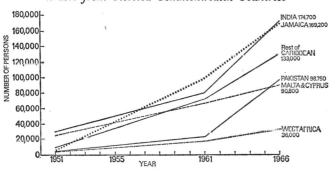

Notes: 1. Figures for 1951 and 1961 are from census reports.

2. Except for West Africa, the 1966 figures included persons under-enumerated in the 1966 10 per cent sample census.

3. Anglo-Indians are not included in the immigrant population of India and Pakistan in 1966 estimates.

* Reproduced from D. Eversley and F. Sukdeo, op. cit. p. 8.

some 91,000 settled.[14] The period 1951 to 1962 saw a large influx of immigrants from the Commonwealth, mainly from the West Indies, India and Pakistan, and Cyprus. The number of coloured immigrants, which was 78,000 in 1951, increased fourfold in ten years and stood at 347,000 in 1961, and between 1962 and 1967 a further 300,000 coloured people settled here.[15] Figure 1 provides some details as to the growth of numbers up to 1966.

Geographical Distribution

In a highly industrialized and urbanized country like Britain it is not at all surprising to find immigrants living mainly in the urban centres. These do provide the most numerous opportunities for employment to the indigenous population as well as to the immigrants. What does stand out as a special pattern concerning immigrants is their higher degree of concentration in urban centres as compared with the rest of the population. By concentration is meant both the higher percentages in the largest towns and the segregation within these towns into minority enclaves, often called ghettos.

To illustrate the above the following comparative figures are of interest. Of the total population of Britain 44 per cent live in the seven largest conurbations[16] and 53 per cent of the population live in towns of 50,000 or more.[17] However, 89 per cent of West Indians, 84 per cent of Pakistanis and 77 per cent of Indians live in such towns.[18] Taking the coloured groups together the 1961 Census showed that 71 per cent were concentrated in six major conurbations, and that of the total 47 per cent were in London and 14 per cent in the West Midlands. There were some variations as between ethnic groups in that the proportion of Pakistanis in the Yorkshire conurbation was relatively high and that fewer West Indians than Indians and Pakistanis lived outside the conurbations. But the high degree of concentration for coloured minorities as a whole continued to show itself in the 1966 Census.[19]

Within the cities the coloured groups are to be found in large numbers in particular districts. In London, Brent, Hackney, Lambeth, Haringey, Islington and Hammersmith have the largest numbers.[20] Both in respect of concentrating heavily in the largest cities and in being very numerous in some areas closer to city centres, the coloured minorities show patterns of distribution very similar to those of other minority groups. Ruth Glass and others have shown, for example, that the distribution of West Indians in London and Birmingham follows the paths taken by the Irish in these towns.[21] Of course the Irish have a much longer history of settlement in British cities and their preference in the nineteenth century for Liverpool and Glasgow has shifted more recently to the industrially expanding areas such as Birmingham and Coventry. In London itself the earliest settlements around St Giles and Holborn had given way by the turn of the century to strong concentrations in the dockland areas of East London, and by the middle of this century to large Irish communities in West London, particularly in Brent, Camden, Paddington, Kensington and Hammersmith. In certain parts of Brent the concentrations are very heavy: nearly $24\frac{1}{2}$ per cent of the total population of Kilburn are Irish-born, over 22 per cent in Mapesbury and 19 per cent in Cricklewood. Of all the Irish in Britain one third live in London, over $10\frac{1}{2}$ per cent in South East Lancashire and Merseyside, and over 8 per cent in the West Midlands.[22]

The story for Poles, Jews, Cypriots and other minorities is similar. It is known that nearly 40,000 Poles, that is one third of the entire Polish community, live in London. Within London the Poles first settled in poorer districts like Paddington and Lambeth, where they could get accommodation cheaply. As they improved their conditions they moved into better areas such as South Kensington where the Earl's Court Road was nicknamed 'The Polish Corridor'.[23] In other parts of the country Poles are particularly numerous in Lancashire with about 14,000, the West Riding of Yorkshire with about 13,000, Staffordshire, Gloucestershire and Warwickshire. The largest Polish communities outside London are in Manchester, Bradford, Birmingham, Bristol, Glasgow and Edinburgh.[24]

The Italians, the Cypriots, the Chinese and the West Africans are mainly concentrated in London. The Italians particularly in the Soho and Clerkenwell districts; but there is also a large Italian community in Bedford numbering between six and seven thousand.[25] The Chinese are more spread out but they too, after concentrating in earlier periods in dockland areas, now tend to cluster nearer central city areas. The Cypriots are heavily concentrated in London, particularly in the Islington, Camden Town and Finsbury Park areas. In 1961 there were 63 per cent living in the metropolis and the percentage rises to 83 if we add the Home Counties. Another town with a fairly large Cypriot community is Liverpool. The West Africans are mainly in London and especially in Wandsworth, Kensington and various parts of North-West London.[26]

As for the Jews 68 per cent live in the metropolis and 88 per cent are concentrated in the six largest cities: London (280,000) Manchester (35,000), Leeds (20,000), Glasgow (13,000), Liverpool (7,000) and Birmingham (6,000). The most significant trend in the last two decades concerning the distribution of the Jewish population has been the rapid move of the Jews from the urban central areas, the old ghetto quarters, to the new suburban districts around the big conurbations. The trek to the 'green belts' has now become extremely pronounced: former well-known Jewish areas such as the East End of London, Cheetham in Manchester, and Chapeltown in Leeds, have lost their Jewish inhabitants who have moved *en masse* to the new areas. London now has large concentrations of Jews in Edgware and Ilford; a large proportion of the Jews in Manchester have moved to Prestwich and Whitefield, and the majority of the Jews of Leeds are to be found in Moortown and Alwoodley. The outflow from the older districts has resulted, however, in a somewhat wider spread of the Jewish population to more distant places, where Jews have settled in a more scattered fashion in predominantly non-Jewish areas. It is interesting to note here that of the 102 organized Jewish communities in England and Wales, 81 are small, containing less than 500 Jews. Even the largest community of London with its 280,000 Jews has lost its compactness of the pre-war days when 100,000 Jews lived in the East End. But Jews still live in a contiguous fashion in large numbers in North-West London, where even in the newer suburbs such as Edgware the 8,000 Jews constitute 40 per cent of the total population of the area.[27]

Whilst it is true that like the Jews other minorities, in particular the Poles and the Irish,[28] have been prone to move out of first areas of settlement and take up residence in smaller concentrations nearer suburbs, the evidence for the coloured minorities is not as yet clear. The 1966 Census did point to greater dispersal among Jamaicans and Pakistanis when compared with the 1961 Census,[29] but it is claimed that figures showing such a trend are misleading. The argument is that because the 1966 Census was a 10 per cent sample Census and because of the degree of under-enumeration of immigrants the figures are not reliable. Furthermore the figures do not include children born in this country to coloured parents. If anything, some experts claim, concentration among West Indians, Indians and Pakistanis has become heavier.[30]

The figures concerning concentration tell different stories according to the 'areas' one takes. Thus at 'borough' level the concentrations do not appear very heavy, the highest in London for West Indians being 6 per cent of the population of Hackney and something like $5\frac{1}{2}$ per cent for Brent and Lambeth. But at 'ward' level the picture changes and one gets over 21 per cent of West Indians in Kensal Rise and $24\frac{1}{2}$ per cent of Asians in Northcote (Ealing).[31] Similarly, in certain wards in Birmingham, such as Soho, the West Indians accounted for 10 per cent of the population in 1961 and Philip Jones also points to much heavier clusters for other parts of Birmingham.[32] Some of the identified clusters with high percentages of coloured immigrants in 1961 were Summerfield Park and Calthorpe Park with over 18 per cent each, Handsworth with nearly 16 per cent and several areas like Balsall Heath, Aston and Sparkbrook with between 11 per cent and 15 per cent. These are percentages of the total populations of the areas. The concentrations appear even stronger if we consider these clusters as percentages of the total coloured population of Birmingham. This shows that 'eleven relatively small areas of the city containing only 9·4 per cent of the city's population account for over 60 per cent of the coloured immigrants'.[33] Similarly, thirteen local authority areas, mostly

London boroughs, accounted for 56 per cent of the total Jamaican population of this country.[34] Ruth Glass maintains, however, that although there are these dense concentrations they do not constitute 'ghettos'. 'The images of Notting Hill and Brixton as the "Harlems" of London are still far from reality.'[35]

TABLE 2.2: *Distribution of Immigrants in Selected London Boroughs 1966**

Percentages of Total Population in Borough

	Irish	Asian	West Indian	African	Cypriot & Maltese
Barnet	3·25	1·50	0·38	0·63	0·64
Brent	8·64	2·16	5·53	0·84	0·53
Camden	7·71	2·67	1·46	1·26	1·98
Ealing	4·85	3·56	1·55	0·36	0·26
Hackney	3·63	1·46	6·00	0·70	1·54
Hammersmith	8·37	1·68	4·53	0·88	0·68
Haringey	4·31	1·61	4·22	0·88	3·34
Islington	5·05	0·72	3·25	1·39	3·26
Kensington & Chelsea	6·42	3·64	2·16	1·68	1·58
Lambeth	4·59	1·45	5·19	1·09	0·80
Southwark	4·00	0·41	2·92	0·36	1·31
Tower Hamlets	1·35	2·26	1·83	0·18	1·38
Wandsworth	4·06	1·67	3·48	0·99	0·40
Westminster	7·32	2·53	2·84	1·35	0·70
GLC TOTAL	3·70	1·53	1·98	0·56	0·76

* Adapted from Table 1, *Race Today*, Dec. 1969, p. 228.[36]

Yet whilst segregated 'coloured quarters' in the American style do not exist in Britain the concentrations are very substantial and it will be interesting to see in the next decade or so whether the coloured minorities, who are the latest arrivals,

will be able to imitate the other minority groups in moving
out on a big scale from their first areas of settlement. So far,
their pattern of settlement has been basically similar to that of
the other minorities. Their areas of residence do in fact often
overlap with those of other minority groups;[37] 'coincidence' of
settlement for minorities is a natural process in the kind of
urban industrial society we are concerned with. As we shall see
in the next chapter, dealing with occupations and housing,
immigrants are as a rule given opportunities for work at the
lower end of the occupational scale and for housing in the
decaying areas in the older parts nearer the centres of cities.
Thus the Birmingham clusters identified earlier as containing
high percentages of coloured immigrants also contain very
large concentrations of Irish-born persons, although the latter
are to be found also in substantial numbers in the newer suburbs. But well over 50 per cent of the Irish live in a 'middle

FIGURE 2: *Ecological Zones in Industrial Conurbations*

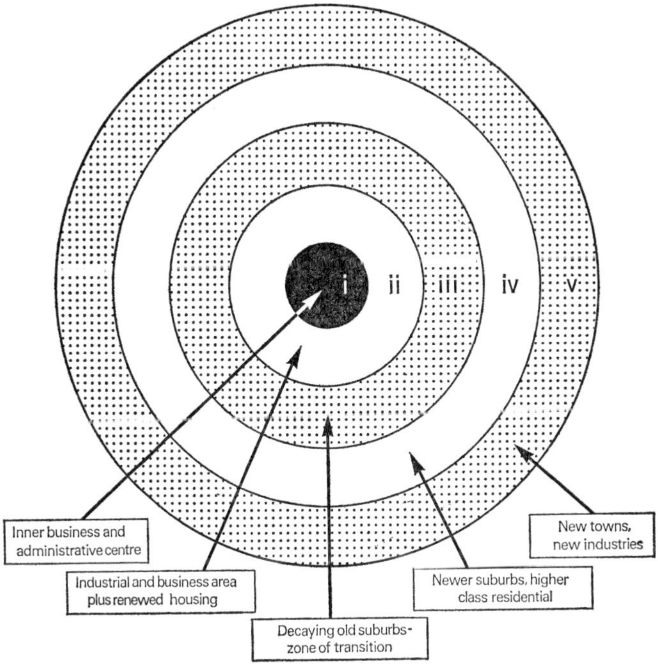

Inner business and
administrative centre

Industrial and business area
plus renewed housing

Decaying old suburbs-
zone of transition

Newer suburbs, higher
class residential

New towns,
new industries

43

ring' of the city covering mainly poorer districts.[38] As for the West Indians generally in the country, Ceri Peach shows clearly how they have acted as a replacement population. He says:

Geographically, they have been drawn to those regions which, in spite of demand for labour, have not been able to attract much net population from other parts of the country. In towns they are proportionately twice as numerous in those that lost population between 1951 and 1961 as in those which have increased. They have gone to the decreasing urban cores of expanding industrial regions.[39]

If we visualize industrial conurbations in Britain as composed of zones represented by five wide concentric rings,[40] labelled in Figure 2, we can expect to find the newer minorities clustering primarily in Zone III but spilling into Zone II; the older established minorities will be found mainly in Zones III and IV; and the indigenous population in Zones I, II, IV and V.

Age, Sex and Fertility

Immigration, the chief progenitor of minority groups, is not a tidy transplantation of groups of people in their entirety. The process, because of its riskiness and the need to adjust to new conditions, results in a selection in the first place of immigrants who are more mobile and have fewer responsibilities, usually single able-bodied young men. Once this *avant garde* is reasonably established their dependants, that is parents, siblings, spouses, children and other relatives, join them. This is not to say that single girls, young couples and families with children will not be found among the earlier wave of immigrants. But a preponderance of younger people and men in particular can be expected.

As a consequence of this special selection process the age distribution, sex ratio, marriage rates, fertility pattern and death rates are all bound to be affected and to differ from such demographic characteristics in the general population. The differences will be felt for many years. In addition, environmental factors imbibed by immigrants in their countries of

44

origin, and cultural factors, which are often transmitted to successive generations in the minority groups, will exert special pressures on such groups.

As the existing data for the demographic characteristics of minority groups are rather sketchy, or in some cases not available at all, we take only age, sex and fertility to illustrate the differences. Some knowledge of these factors is essential even for the most rudimentary attempts to project minority populations.

A large-scale survey carried out in 1961 among Commonwealth immigrants covering the Southern Irish, West Indians, Australians, New Zealanders, Indians, Pakistanis and Cypriots found that 'More than three-quarters of the immigrants were male, and there was a strong preponderance of the younger age groups, 62 per cent of all respondents being between the ages of 18 and 34, and 83 per cent less than 45 years old.' This compares with only 62 per cent under 45 in the general population of England and Wales (1961 Census). Just over half the respondents were married which compares with 73 per cent of the population of England and Wales (for those over 19 years of age). The survey also showed that, with the exception of the Australasians, at least half in each of the other groups were in intermediate positions in their families, a factor suggesting that the immigrants originated mainly from large families.[41]

Among the Jewish immigrants at the end of the last century youthfulness was similarly in evidence. The age-distribution among the men shows that the great majority were in their prime of life: 26 per cent under 20; 63 per cent between 21 and 40; 10 per cent between 41 and 60; and 0·5 per cent over 60. Of all the Jewish immigrants at that time 55 per cent were men, 25 per cent women, and 20 per cent children. These figures may show that many of the Jewish immigrants did come with their families,[42] although it was more usual for single men to pioneer ahead.[43] By the 1950s the age distribution of Jews became a more normal one and resembled rather more closely the age distribution in the general population. In the age group 0–14 the Jews had 20·4 per cent and the total population of the country 22·8 per cent; the percentage in group 15–34 was

25·8 for both populations; and the figures for those aged 35 and over were respectively 53 per cent and 51·4 per cent.[44] Again a study of fertility trends among Jews showed that the larger families of the first decades of this century sharply declined. According to one estimate the number of children per Jewish family changed from 3 in 1921 to 1·4 in 1950.[45] The baby boom of the late 1950s and early 1960s showed itself among Jews as in the general population.[46]

The statistics for the Irish show that in some respects they follow the general pattern for immigrants; in other respects they do not. The preponderance of young people comes up again: 49 per cent were between 20 and 40 years old in 1951 which compares with a national figure of 29 per cent for the same age range.[47] This reflects the continuous nature of Irish immigration, as does also the fact that the proportion of married people among the Irish is lower than that in the general population. However, the sex ratio has changed over the last century. Whilst up to 1890 with the Irish, as with other immigrants, males were more numerous than females, since that date the situation has been reversed. In England, though not in Scotland and Wales, females outnumber males among the Irish-born. This is particularly true of the South East and of London where in 1951 the ratio of females to males was 1,340; 1,000.[48] The fertility rate for Irish women was found to be rather high in a study carried out in Birmingham in the early 1960s. At the age of 30 Irish women had had 3·4 pregnancies compared with 2·1 pregnancies for English women.[49]

In the case of the West Indians, as with the Irish, the percentage of women immigrants is remarkably high. The high proportion of Jamaican women is particularly noticeable in the London conurbation. The attraction to London of large numbers of women from the general population as well as from immigrant groups seems to be due to the existence of more high-status jobs suitable for women, in contrast, say, to Birmingham where occupations in the metal industries are more suitable for men. Even so, there is still an overall preponderance of men immigrants among the coloured groups, although this male dominance has declined since 1961:

63 per cent of the net increase in the coloured population between 1951 and 1961 was male compared with only 56 per cent between 1961 and 1966.[50] The evidence on age structure shows again the dominance of the young in the case of coloured minorities. In 1961 29 per cent were under 15 years of age; 61 per cent between 15 and 44; and 10 per cent 45 and over. The respective figures for the total population were: 23 per cent, 40 per cent and 37 per cent. By 1966 the coloured groups had a higher percentage than in 1961 of those below the age of 15, a swing mainly due to the West Indian group which had a remarkable increase in its child population.[51] We shall discuss below in greater detail fertility trends among coloured minorities.

The basic statistical information for some of the smaller minorities is very scanty, but what information is available does point to certain of the special features described above. The Polish community in 1951, for instance, had 74·4 per cent males and 25·6 per cent females. The bulk of the community consisted of adults of working age, mainly in the 18–59 group. The proportion of children under 18 was low; estimates in the 1950s ranging from 11 per cent to 19·4 per cent.[52] The Cypriots had twice as many males as females in 1951 but by 1961 the ratio of males to females was 5:4. The youthfulness of the community was evident. In 1961 there were 37·2 per cent in the age group 0–14; and only 1·6 per cent were aged 65 and over.[53] The male dominated pattern was similarly strongly in evidence among the Chinese for many decades, but by 1961 the sex ratio among London's Chinese swung in favour of females.[54]

A rough general pattern among immigrant minority groups can be observed. The preponderance of men and of younger people in general is the main feature, particularly in the earlier stages in the life of a minority: the first waves of settlers. This is usually accompanied by a low marriage rate and birth rate, as well as by a low death rate. There are of course regional variations, where for instance the metropolis has high percentages of females because of the employment opportunities. There are also variations between ethnic groups, but the main features just mentioned do apply on the whole to most of the groups. After the first influx of immigrants the community settles down and its demographic features alter as a result of the following process: dependants join the early settlers, being mainly child-bearing women and children; this brings about a more balanced sex ratio, but it also greatly increases the proportion of children in the minority, so that at a later stage, even if immigration is halted or ceases naturally, the minority is still likely to expand. The expansion will then depend on the fertility of the minority, and the proportion that it will make up of the whole population will be largely determined by the difference between its own fertility trend and that of the indigenous population.

We should, therefore, now consider the indications regarding fertility trends and compare the relevant statistics for the general population and minority groups.[55] But a true comparison is hardly possible for the following reasons. The fertility rate is

the totality of births in relation to the female population and its determinants are: 1) The age structure of the female population – the higher the proportion of women in child-bearing age groups, the higher the fertility rate is likely to be. 2) The ages at which women marry – the younger they do so, the higher the overall fertility rate is likely to be. 3) Social class and cultural factors.[56]

Considering this definition and its implications it stands to reason that in order to be able to compare fertility trends one must match comparable age groups of women of comparable marriage durations.

There is no sophisticated study of this kind as yet available. To produce statistics through the kind of survey carried out for the Ministry of Health and Social Security in the spring of 1969 is in many ways misleading. The survey showed, for instance, that in some London boroughs the number of coloured births was very high: 1 in 3 in Lambeth and Brent, 1 in 4 in Islington, and 1 in 5 in Wandsworth. Again, some towns had high figures: 1 in 4.5 in Wolverhampton, 1 in 5 in Huddersfield and 1 in 6 in Birmingham and Leicester. Such information merely reflects the high immigrant concentrations in certain areas, which is clearly shown by the fact that other places had far lower figures: Bristol and Sheffield 1 in 19, the London boroughs of Tower Hamlets 1 in 10 and Lewisham 1 in 13.[57] The Registrar-General's figures for the middle half of 1969, however, show the general increase in the number of births to immigrant parents. These represented nearly 12 per cent of the total births in the country. The biggest single group of births was to immigrant mothers from the Republic of Ireland. This was 3 per cent, followed by 2·5 per cent to mothers from India and Pakistan, and 2 per cent to those from the West Indies.[58]

But the baby-boom statistics must be read in conjunction with certain facts regarding the determinants of fertility as set out above. Thus, coloured immigrant women are in larger numbers in the younger child-bearing ages than are English women; for instance many more West Indian women than English women are under thirty. This means that the West Indians produce more children per thousand of their population than do the English; and it also means that more of the English women will have completed their families. Hence comparability of crude birth figures per thousand of the population are not useful, just as information on the proportion of coloured children in a particular area does not help one to understand the true situation.

The 1969 Report on Race Relations suggests, however, that the biases can be removed 'by concentrating merely on families which have children under 15 years of age', for this keeps our attention on comparable groups. According to the evidence from such data the families of immigrant groups are larger by about one third than those of the English population.[59] But the data used was not extensive enough to place this finding on a firm basis. It must, therefore, be regarded as preliminary and tentative information.

Population Projections

Forecasting population trends is a hazardous business because of the unforeseen circumstances that may affect fertility, migration and mortality. The predictions of demographers have at times been falsified, despite the considerable data and research

c

concerning the general population.[60] Now when we wish to forecast minority populations the exercise becomes even more difficult because more 'unknowns' are added, such as the possibility of quite drastic cultural changes, which may lead to widespread and effective family limitation.

Despite the difficulties, forecasts have been made especially for the newer growing immigrant groups. Most attention has been given to the coloured minorities although other groups, notably the Cypriots, the Italians and the Irish, are also growing substantially. So far as the coloured groups are concerned the projections take account of three streams of people: those already resident in the United Kingdom at a particular date; those eligible to enter the country as dependants; and voucher holders, that is new immigrants coming to jobs who themselves will be joined by their dependants.[61] Using figures for the late 1960s to calculate its projections, the Report on British Race Relations estimates that by 1986 there will be between two and two and a quarter million people in coloured minority groups resident in this country.[62] To arrive at this estimate several assumptions were made, the more important being: that fertility among coloured immigrant women will be twice that of English women; that the inflow of dependants, particularly from India and Pakistan, will be considerable; that the current rate of voucher issues will be continued; and that there will be no return migration.[63]

The assumption about the fertility of coloured women is on the generous side. It is true that in 1963 a study in Birmingham showed that at the age of 45 Indian and Pakistani women had had an average of between 5 and 6 pregnancies, West Indian women 5 pregnancies, and English women 3 pregnancies. These differences may not persist, however, as immigrants coming mainly from rural backgrounds become influenced by Western urban family planning habits. Thus, the same study also found that the 'ideal family' size chosen by immigrants came close to that chosen by the English. The latter chose 3.2 and so did the West Indians, whilst the Indians and Pakistanis chose 3.4. There were also indications that family planning would spread among immigrants.[64] It should be remembered that there are precedents for this both from other minority groups and from the English population itself.

As the English population became more thoroughly urbanized, the average number of children per family was reduced from 5·8, for those who married in the decade 1870–9, to 3·4 for those who began their marriages in 1900–9, and to 2·2 for those who married in 1925.[65] This notable reduction, achieved by the spread of birth control, did, however, take eighty years. The Jewish minority achieved the same results and according to estimates the contemporary Jewish family is even smaller than the English one, with only 1·4 children per Jewish family in the 1950s. This may be due to the Jewish population having a larger proportion in the higher socio-economic groups, since fertility does vary between such groups. The fact still remains that the Family Limitation Survey of the Royal Commission on Population, 1949, found that a higher proportion of Jewish women, married in the inter-war period, applied birth control than was the case in any other religious group, and also that Jews, compared to Protestants and Catholics, had the highest proportion using appliance methods.[66] Even among Catholics approval of birth control was on the increase, a fact that would naturally affect such minorities as the Irish, the Italians and the Poles. Thus, the Population Investigation Committee's Marriage Survey 1959–60 found that whereas among the Catholics married prior to 1930 only 18·5 per cent fully approved of birth control, among those married after 1950 39·4 per cent fully approved.[67]

The same trend towards more birth control is noticeable also in coloured minorities: among West Indians, for instance there has been a progressive decline in fertility since 1963, the peak year – the reduction amounting to 25 per cent by 1967. This evidence comes from Birmingham, and it is stressed that the reduction could not have taken place naturally, that is by a decline in fecundity. This occurs among women in their late thirties whilst the median age among West Indian women was thirty in 1966.[68] The decline must have been induced by the increasing use of birth control methods. Fertility among Indians and Pakistanis has still been on the increase but more family planning is likely to occur among these groups too, as knowledge about methods increases.[69]

Concerning the future arrivals of dependants and voucher holders the likely position was calculated by Eversley and Sukdeo and has the following salient features. In 1967 48,000 coloured people came to Britain of which total 72 per cent were dependants. The estimates show that with the existing coloured population plus the voucher holders yet to enter the country, the number of dependants joining them after 1967 is likely to rise to 236,000. If the 1967 rate of arrivals were maintained the bulk of dependants would settle here within the next five years.[70] Alternatively these arrivals would spread over more years. The early indication is that this would in fact happen, as those coming in under the 1968 Commonwealth Immigrants Act in the first nine months of 1969 numbered only 29,150.[71] A comparison of the first quarter in each of the years of 1968, 1969 and 1970 shows the continuing downward trend. The figures for total admissions of Commonwealth immigrants were respectively: 13,539, 10,118 and 6,728, the last being the lowest figure since records were kept in 1962.[72]

The voucher holders themselves, of whom the maximum number allowed in per annum is 7,500, are coming in at the rate of 5,000 per annum. At the same time there is a substantial return migration, particularly among professionally qualified persons. Between 1962 and 1964 1,935 Commonwealth-born doctors entered with vouchers, but in the same period 1,507 left Britain.[73] The total return migration to India, Pakistan and the West Indies ran at the average of 14,000 a year in 1966 and 1967.[74] The future reflux of immigrants will depend on the relative economic and social conditions here and in their original home countries. There are also a few minor points to be mentioned. Illegal entry is minute: it was officially estimated in 1969 to be a few hundred per year. Students, as a potential source of new settlers, are becoming less significant than in the recent past. The numbers are on the decline due to the higher fees charged to overseas students. Finally, it is not possible to say to what extent advantage

52

would be taken of the one loophole in the present legislation, that is bringing over dependants through newly 'arranged' marriages.

Considering all of the above points there can be little doubt that the forecast given above of a maximum of two and a half million coloured Britons by 1986 is reasonable and is likely to err on the positive side. This projection would mean that with an estimated general population of nearly 65 million there would be 3·8 per cent of coloured people in this country compared with 2·4 per cent in 1968. Earlier forecasts have made assumptions about net inflow and fertility which constituted even more liberal allowances and arrived, therefore, at higher figures. The Economist Intelligence Unit estimated in 1964 that there would be 3·2 million coloured people in Britain in the year 2002 in a total population which would have grown by that time to 72·6 million – a proportion of 4·4 per cent. In 1967 the Ministry of Health gave an estimate of 3·5 million coloured people in 1985 which in a total population of over 60 million would amount to 5·8 per cent.[75] These percentage estimates would be even higher if we accepted the lower figure for the total population of Britain given by R. K. Kelsall for 2001 as sixty-six and a half million.[76] However, projections made at the National Institute of Economic and Social Research for the mid-1980s suggest a more moderately sized coloured population than would appear for some of the estimates we mentioned, and more in line with the predictions made by the Report on British Race Relations quoted above. The annual inflow of coloured immigrants was put at 30,000, at which rate the coloured population would increase to 2·6 million by 1986, that is by 4·4 per cent per annum. But the researchers at the NIESR also considered the possibilities of under-enumeration and re-emigration and, therefore, state: 'Assuming, say, under-enumeration of the order of 10 per cent in 1966, the projected 1985 numbers would be about 3 per cent greater [than their estimate of over two and a half million]. In contrast, an allowance for re-emigration would greatly reduce the projections. Should re-emigration occur at the rate of 2 per cent per annum, it would cut the projected rate of growth (of " old" and " new" immigrants) from 4·2 per cent to

2·3 per cent per annum, yielding a 1985 coloured population of the order of one and three quarter million.'[77]

The variations in the projections, all of which are on the generous side, suggest that the coloured minorities may number by the beginning of the next century between two and a quarter and three and a half million, representing roughly between 4 and 6 per cent of the total population. Other minorities likely to grow are the Cypriots, the Italians and the Irish; they all have high fertility rates, and in the case of the Irish there is also a continued replenishment which is at a sufficiently high level[78] to counteract the rather faster process of assimilation among them. Some minorities, however, show definite signs of a decline in their numbers. The Jews, who were estimated to number between 450,000 and half a million in the immediate post-war period, numbered only 410,000 by 1965.[79] Rather low fertility, intermarriage and a small outward flow, mainly of younger people to Israel, have taken their toll. The number of Poles in the country has similarly been on the decline. In 1949 there were 157,000 Poles in Britain. By 1954 their numbers had dropped to 130,000 mainly through emigration to the USA.[80] With no further influx of Poles and as a result of the inroads of assimilation, their numbers are likely to drop further.

The overall picture, then, is one of a decline in the sizes of the older minorities, excluding the Irish, and a substantial but by no means phenomenal increase in the newer minority groups, with a tendency for this increase to level off among the coloured minorities towards the end of the century.

3   The Scene in Britain: Official and Unofficial Attitudes

For many centuries Britain has been a favourite asylum for refugees and a country of increased opportunities for immigrants. Wave after wave of hunted and poverty-stricken men have sought refuge on these shores, and more often than not have been accepted. Britain has a very long history of permitting the settlement of minority groups. But its history also shows that there was a two-way process at work; the influx was often more than matched by an outflow of Britain's population. Thus between 1871 and 1931 Britain had a net outflow, through migration mainly to the Empire, of over three million people.[1]

Yet despite the comparatively tolerant atmosphere in Britain, popular resentment at the establishment of minority groups has usually been a feature of life in this country. There has also been a good measure of prejudice at a semi-official level. On the whole, however, influenced by its policy of free trade and its industrial success in the nineteenth century, Britain maintained officially a free movement of populations until the beginning of this century. This did not prevent the existence of certain antagonisms directed against newcomers. One writer in 1788 spoke of 'a little race of mulattoes, mischievous as monkeys, and infinitely more dangerous'.[2] The Irishman was much abused. *The Times* in the 1840s branded him as indolent[3] and Friedrich Engels, the working-class revolutionary thinker, was able to say of the Irish immigrant that 'his crudity places him little above the savage'.[4] Much of the anti-Irish propaganda branding them as lazy, diseased and criminal was broadcast by no lesser persons than doctors and lawyers, despite the lack of real evidence to back up such generalizations; and this was further fanned by Anglo-Irish religious discord.[5]

The Jews as a growing minority group towards the end of the nineteenth century did not fare any better. Although the English humanitarian tradition detested the absolutist régimes of the Russian Tsars under whom the Jews suffered, a speaker denouncing the oppression in the 1880s remarked none the less that this brought to England 'a great number of Jews to take the bread out of our citizens' mouths'.[6] At the end of the century Charles Booth added to the growing criticism of immigrant Jews. He described them as 'possessed of many first-class virtues, [but] deficient in that highest and latest development of human sentiment – social morality'.[7] In Parliament there were some members lobbying for restricting immigration and the Government benches were being strongly influenced by both milder and more rabid propaganda. Most of the pronouncements, on the whole irrational and unsubstantiated, were remarkably similar to the statements and views voiced in the 1960s regarding coloured immigrants. The Jews at the turn of the century were said to be below English standards 'both in physique and in moral and social customs'.[8] They were said to be dirty, a burden on rates and taxes, spreading disease and criminality. Like the Irish they were accused of providing cheap labour and thus bringing about unemployment among English workers. Resentment was also felt about the cohesiveness of their community and it was feared that they might change the character of some central city areas, particularly the East End of London.

Most of these charges were exhaustively investigated by a number of official inquiries and were, by and large, refuted. V. D. Lipman observes that these inquiries disproved most charges, but not that relating to overcrowding and the consequent rise in rents.[9] The 1888 House of Commons Select Committee on Emigration and Immigration found the Jews moral and inoffensive as citizens but uncleanly in their habits (a factor quite possibly due to overcrowding). In the same year the House of Lords set up a Select Committee on Sweating which reported that 'undue stress has been laid on the injurious effect on wages caused by foreign immigration'. The House of Commons Select Committee and the Board of Trade Reports in 1894 also stressed that the number of immigrants was not as high as claimed and that it gave no cause for alarm. Furthermore the Reports showed that 'few trades were affected by the aliens and that, so far from there being an adverse effect on the conditions and earnings of native workers, new industries had been brought in'.[10] The Board of Trade Reports also found the immigrant Jews to be law-abiding, sober and industrious.

The most important inquiry was undertaken by the Royal Commission appointed in 1902. This concluded that there was no case for excluding immigrants altogether but recommended the imposition of controls, which eventually led to the passing of the 1905 Aliens Act. This Act, which reduced Jewish immigration into this country to a trickle, was defended simply on the grounds that it would be undesirable for the country to have a large minority, however patriotic and industrious they might be.[11] Although Acts of Parliament to check on immigration had been passed previously, in 1793, 1826 and 1836, these were mainly connected with such events as the French Revolution and the Napoleonic Wars, and were not severely restrictionist.[12] The 1905 Act, therefore, marks the first serious step towards restrictionism.

While political and civil liberty had been extended to the Jewish immigrant, the ghetto dweller, whether in East London or the Leeds Leylands, was exposed to the social intolerance of the native population, who boycotted the Jew in respect of the provision of housing and employment, and notices inscribed 'No Jews need apply' were a common sight. The Jews often had to face even physical violence.[13]

The prejudice and discrimination aroused by Irish and Jewish immigrants in the nineteenth century, and the official attitudes expressed by leading personalities and embodied in the laws passed, were repeated in the case of coloured immigrants and even European immigrants in the twentieth century. In the 1920s there was widespread prejudice against the employment of young coloured people in Liverpool and Cardiff.[14] A year earlier the first 'race riot' in Britain took place in Cardiff. The agitation, which expressed fears about competition for work by coloured seamen, involved only small numbers.[15] In 1934 one Member of Parliament had this to say: 'Is it a nice sight as I walk through the south end of the city of Liverpool, to find a black settlement, a black body of men – I am not saying a word about their colour – all doing well, and a white body of men who faced the horrors of war, walking the streets unemployed?'[16] In this connexion it was in fact the Chinese and the East Indians who were singled out by the speaker quoted, but allusions were made at this time to the possibility of 'repatriating' the coloured population of Britain to the West Coast of Africa.[17] Little also mentions the difficulty that coloured people had before the Second World War in obtaining accommodation and work and he concluded that 'a fairly strong body of colour prejudice exists in Britain, despite its lack of sanction or support by the law'.[17]

There have been a number of attempts to assess more accurately the extent to which Britain is prejudiced against minorities. Several surveys have been carried out by social scientists and by social research organizations. A PEP report issued in 1967 mentioned the use of situation tests in which matched individuals from different immigrant groups and from the native English population took part to show that immigrants were discriminated against and that the degree of discrimination varied for different groups. In the case of certain services, such as motor insurance, West Indians were discriminated against much more than Indians and Pakistanis, and the least amount of discrimination was felt in this respect by the Cypriots;[18] 23 per cent of them claimed to have suffered from discriminatory practices, whilst the figure for West Indians was 61 per cent. As for private lettings of accommodation, the report showed how the 'No coloureds' – 'Europeans only' bar was applied; its situation tests proved that Hungarians experienced, in this respect, little discrimination as compared with West Indians.[19] The amount of discrimination and prejudice immigrants have to endure seems to vary even by the shade of their skin colour. An earlier PEP report in 1955 reported that 'less than half of the light-skinned West Indian students experienced prejudice as compared with 80 per cent of dark-skinned West Indians'.[20]

European minorities, it appears, are exposed to a smaller dose of discrimination although to be sure they have not managed to escape it altogether. Polish settlers were in fact shocked to find in the early post-war period that there was opposition to their employment in this country.[21] But undoubtedly discrimination against coloured minorities has been far more serious. The degree of discrimination does vary, however, according to different aspects of white-coloured relationships. It has been shown clearly that there is a greater objection to intermarriage between white and coloured than to coloured people living in the same district. In 1961 it was found that 68 per cent of white people disapproved of intermarriage but only 48 per cent said that they would leave their district if many coloured people came to live there.[22] In turn, working with coloured people appears to arouse less antipathy than living with them. One survey in 1961 reported 19 per cent as disliking the idea of working with coloured people and a 1964 survey put the figure at 22 per cent.[23] These figures simply confirm the feasibility of measuring the degree of hostility or acceptance shown to ethnic groups by means of a social-distance scale of the kind developed by E. S. Bogardus.[24] It is apparent from this technique that the crux of the matter when measuring acceptance or rejection exhibited in social relationships is the degree of intimacy involved.[25] The reaction of the British white person in this respect does not differ, therefore, from reactions in other countries as far as we can judge from social-distance measurements. We have little material which shows the British preferences regarding various minority groups. But some British attitudes can be gleaned from a survey of Wolverhampton. Respondents there were most keenly aware of the existence of coloured minorities, but the existence of European groups was also recognized. Such awareness may in part be due to the relative size of groups, but more specific concern regarding their existence was voiced along other criteria. These were primarily the contribution minorities made to the community, and their ability to assimilate in terms of language, religion and social behaviour.[26]

The picture regarding the circumstances in which prejudice and discrimination is fostered or discouraged is not very clear. In 1956 Michael Banton undertook a survey from which he concluded that 'colour prejudice is not widespread in Britain'.[27] He based his assertion on the low figures showing outright prejudice: only 18 per cent objected to coloured people coming to this country; 10 per cent to having them as neighbours; and 6 per cent to working with them.[28] Clifford Hill, who in his 1964 survey obtained much higher figures, came to the conclusion that colour prejudice steadily increased between these dates and seemed to argue that Banton's low figures were the result of interviewing in areas which at the time had hardly any actual experience of coloured people.[29] Yet at the same time Hill found 'a definite correlation between personal acquaintance with coloured people and tolerant attitudes';[30] and he takes the optimistic view that in the very long run more frequent contact and familiarity with coloured people may lessen prejudices against them.[31]

A more recent survey, carried out by Mark Abrams for the comprehensive Report on British Race Relations, has borne out some of Hill's predictions and found that contact modified attitudes in a favourable direction.[32] Its results were based on a large-scale investigation including a national survey as well as separate surveys in two London boroughs and three county boroughs all with sizeable groups of immigrants. The overall figures show that 10 per cent of the white population in Britain is strongly prejudiced, 17 per cent is prejudiced-inclined, 38 per cent tolerant-inclined, and 35 per cent tolerant.[33] A finer analysis of the material showed that women, younger people and especially those who received full-time education to a sixth-form standard, showed an incidence of prejudice below average. However, the picture is still far from clear. Whilst the figures seem encouraging when compared with a survey taken ten years earlier (see table), and it is maintained that 'there seems to be a trend for general views on major policy issues affecting the individual to become more favourable', this is qualified by the observation that 'when respondents are asked to consider situations in which they are *personally concerned* [my italics] they have been inclined over the ten years to express less favourable views'.[34] The latter point is at variance with the actual figures of the survey.

TABLE 3.1: *The Extent of Prejudice, 1958 and 1968*[35]

	1958 Glass Gallup %	1968 Rose-Abrams %
Tolerant	19·4	35
Tolerant-inclined	31·2	38
Prejudiced-inclined	36·8	17
Prejudiced	12·6	10

Some experts in the field have criticized the Abrams survey for underestimating the extent to which prejudices prevail. It has been claimed that there were some serious faults in the technique employed to measure prejudice.[36] Considering that the survey also showed that three-quarters of the sample agreed with Enoch Powell's views on race relations,[37] it can be safely assumed that the prejudiced categories, both the more hostile and those only inclined to be prejudiced are far larger than those given by Abrams.

A balanced view regarding British attitudes to immigrants would show, however, that xenophobia has not been the mark all the time or in all circumstances. During the Second World War Jewish children, refugees from Nazi Europe, found comfort in Gentile homes.[38] The Hungarians in 1956 were on the whole favourably received.[39] Intermarriage between the English and members of minorities is another phenomenon showing relationships not marked by prejudice. The rate of intermarriage is still very low although in the case of the Jews and Gentiles it is undoubtedly on the increase.[40] And in some areas, such as Liverpool, intermarriage between white and coloured is more than minimal.[41] More illustrations of favourable attitudes alongside unfavourable ones will be found in the context of organized opinion, a fact that we shall now consider.

Organized Opinion and Action

In this section we look at the attitudes expressed in an organized context: by political parties, racist groups, organizations devoted to achieve greater harmony, the Church, the Press and other bodies such as Trade Unions.

The record of the major political parties and most of their supporters could be assessed as showing their attitudes to have been flexible; in a more critical appraisal one would, however, describe the policies and utterances as muddled. The uncertainty is not surprising: Britain's role on the twentieth-century world scene has been changing rapidly, from that of a mother country at the head of an Empire to the first among equals in a Commonwealth of Nations,[42] and latterly to a possible partner in a new European federation. Attitudes to immigration and immigrants at the organized political level have been inextricably bound up with such changes and all that is implied in economic terms as well as in terms of power politics. Another factor has usually been the need to keep an eye in the short run on forthcoming elections.

The uncertainty is reflected in the widely different stands taken by politicians who in other respects were at the same end of the political spectrum. Thus at the time of the big debate preceding the 1905 Aliens Act, two Liberals with Socialist sympathies and both basically opposing the Bill diverged widely in their attitudes towards Jews. One fell flatly into blatant anti-semitism when attacking 'the rich Jew' whilst the other had this to say:

I am afraid that in this country . . . there has been an agitation kindled and fanned and that an anti-Jewish feeling has been aroused. Those who read the newspapers which support this bill cannot help seeing what their tone is. The faults which are set down against the Jews are caused by persecution in the past . . . The principle of the right of asylum, strong as it is, in the case of Jews ought to apply with double strength to everyone holding Christian principles, as a proper exchange for the hateful and shameful system of persecution.[43]

The campaign for restrictionism continued after the First World War. The anti-alien lobby gained predominance in the Tory Party and although in 1919 the Labour Party voted against extending the Act for peacetime, as Paul Foot points out, 'four subsequent Labour Governments have administered the Bill almost without changing it'.[44] The inter-war recession period was not the most favourable for the Jews who were trying to escape to Britain from Nazi Germany. A few days after the 'Crystal Night' pogrom in 1938 the British Government announced plans to cope with a limited number of refugees and called on its allies to investigate together with Britain the possibility of settling refugees in various colonies. The Government proposed to admit some 'selected' adults and a limited number of children to be trained for re-emigration. It was argued that to do more would lead to 'a definite anti-Jewish movement in the country'.[45]

In the post-war period the Polish minority did not fare much better when it experienced some indifference from the Government and antagonism from other quarters. Government departments differed widely in their approach to the Polish minority and the impression the Poles gained was of a policy that discouraged Polish settlement by allowing unbearable living conditions in the camps. At the Trades Union Congress in 1946 much hostility was evinced and the anti-Polish campaign that developed played mainly on the traditional and deep-rooted fear of foreign labour felt by British workers.

The Poles were now presented not only as Fascists and reactionaries living in idleness at the taxpayers' expense; they were now to be thrown in large numbers on the British labour market and they would jeopardize the maintenance of full employment, bring down British workers' living standards or wages, destroy the hard-earned liberties of trade unionists, accentuate the housing shortage and eat food that Britain could hardly spare.[46]

Yet this was at a time when the country was experiencing a shortage of labour and the Government initiated schemes for bringing in European workers to help rebuild the economy. The interesting thing about these workers is that they were brought in *outside* the 1919 Aliens Restriction Act. Paul Foot sees this as sheer cynicism on the part of British politicians, for 'while insisting to some of their own supporters that the Aliens Act must continue, they were prepared, if the economic necessity arose, to move outside the Act'.[47] The worst performance was put up by the two Communist Members of Parliament. Since these Poles were opting out of life dominated by the Soviet Union they were attacked; but the attack was cloaked in chauvinistic terms, reflected in one Communist M.P.'s remark that 'the Poles should get coal in their own country'.[48]

The British Press does not come out with flying colours in its treatment of minorities. Even the 'quality Press' has been embroiled in a disreputable fashion in spreading myths about foreigners and sometimes giving credence to pure fabrication. An editorial in *The Times* observed in 1853 that 'We very much doubt whether in England, or indeed in any free Protestant country, a true Papist [in reference to the Irish] can be a good subject',[49] and it was an article in the same paper in 1920 that gave a tremendous fillip to the forged anti-Semitic document entitled The Protocols of the Elders of Zion.[50] Later in the 1930s the British Press displayed negative attitudes towards refugee Jews from Europe. Its treatment of the numbers involved was casual in the extreme. The estimates given by the *Daily Express* and the *Observer* of the growing Jewish population of Britain were exaggerations and not in accordance with existing statistical data. An even worse aspect of its negative treatment of the situation can be seen in the implications of the line the Press was taking, which has been carefully analysed by Andrew Sharf. He says: 'One basic assumption emerged ... If more Jewish refugees meant, or might eventually mean, more anti-Semitism in host countries, then the cause of anti-Semitism was – the Jew. And since Anti-Semitism, at least in its more virulent form, was clearly wrong and barbarous, the only course was to prevent any notable increase in one's own Jewish population'.[51]

Public opinion, as mirrored by the Press, was one of underlying mild anti-Semitism mixed with a vague humanitarianism.[52] The traumatic events of the Second World War with the genocidal policy of the Nazis changed this to a more tolerant post-war atmosphere, still dotted however, by anti-alien feeling as noted in connexion with the Poles, or by outbursts of anti-Semitism at the time of the Palestine troubles. But the feeling of sympathy towards fellow underdogs characterized for a while much of the attitudes in the Labour and trade union movements towards the new minorities, the coloured immigrants. The anxieties about recession in 1956 gave way to sharp reactions to the 1958 disturbances in Nottingham and Notting Hill. The Labour Party officially opposed the Commonwealth Immigrants Bill in 1961-2, invoking the argument of manpower shortage against restrictionism. In the Conservative camp too there were those who for many years acquiesced in maintaining the *status quo* which allowed Commonwealth immigrants, who were British citizens and hence outside the Aliens Act, to settle in this country. There were two main reasons for the acquiescence: one that the immigration met the demands of industrialists for increased labour supply; the other that politically it was expedient for keeping good relations with members of the newly shaped British Commonwealth. The latter was also the ground on which some of the Press opposed the Commonwealth Immigrants Bill. Yet as the number of immigrants was increasing so the restrictionists were gaining ground. Equivocation largely disappeared in the brief period of 1962-4. By 1965 both the popular and the serious Press were harassing the Labour Government for failing to tighten up the controls introduced in 1962, and the overall feeling in the major political parties, as well as in the Trade Unions and the Government itself was that further measures to stop the influx had become necessary.[53]

The question is why this rapid shift took place. Was it that Britain's economic and political conditions were clearly changing? The boom of the 'never had it so good' period was certainly over, and there were signs that the Commonwealth was losing importance and cohesiveness. (Parallel with this was the developing interest in the Common Market.) However the strongest pressure for further restriction was created by a typical 'vicious circle' situation. As restrictive legislation was being proposed, the would-be immigrants hurried along to enter before the doors were closed. This swelled their ranks and multiplied the problems, particularly in so far as housing was concerned. The conditions were then ripe for more agitation on behalf of those wanting a total ban on immigration, which in turn would bring about a great deal of adverse publicity and popular feeling against immigration of panic proportions, the best example of which was the London dockers' march to Parliament in the summer of 1968. Here was a march of left-wing Trade Unionists in support of the views of right-wing politicians indulging in scapegoatism at a time of economic trouble; for many people this was reminiscent of the unsettled period in Germany between the wars. The Government response would then be one of further action in order, one would suppose, not to lose popular support. But it is interesting to note that evidence from a number of studies suggests that apart from exceptional situations as in Smethwick the Labour Party was not very much harmed electorally as a result of the immigration issue.[54] Nevertheless more rigid legislative measures were introduced by the Labour Government as evidenced by the White Paper on Immigration of 1965. From Sheila Patterson's detailed description of events it appears that by this time a convergence of opinion between the major parties had taken place[55] in respect of immigration control.

At the same time it is true that the Labour Government kept its pledge to bring in anti-discrimination measures, which took the form of the Race Relations Act 1965 outlined below. This was the first major legislation designed to achieve harmony in race relations and to help immigrants. But some action had been taken in former years both at central and local government level, and particularly by non-governmental bodies. Looking back from the 1930s we find for instance the Academic Assistance Council created at the London School of Economics to aid Jewish refugee scholars.[56] To help the European Voluntary Workers in 1948 the Central Co-Ordinating Committee of Refugee Welfare Organizations was established. This was aided by the Government and so was the British Council for Aid to Refugees.[57]

In regard to coloured immigrants some commentators have alleged that there had been official uncertainty and inaction. Nicholas Deakin feels that such criticism has not been entirely just; that the outward appearance of indifference of the 1950s and early 1960s is deceptive.[58] Certainly local authorities have had the power to appoint special workers or to form consultative committees to enhance the welfare of immigrants in local communities. Such special workers have been appointed for instance by the Education Committee of Nottingham City Council and the Public Health Department of Westminster City Council. Nadine Peppard reported in 1965 that there were twenty-eight consultative committees throughout the country. Although such committees have sprung up mainly since the influx of coloured immigrants, they do play a role in integrating other minorities too, such as the Greek Cypriots in the case of the Haringey Commonwealth Citizens' Consultative Committee. The task of such committees is mainly to co-ordinate the work of bodies which help to integrate the minorities. Nadine Peppard sets out roughly the areas of inquiry that such committees are liable to be involved in. These are: 'Assessment of the number and nationalities of coloured people in the area, housing problems, social activities, informal language tuition, participation of coloured people in the civic life of the town, employment problems, reduction of racial tension where it exists'.[59]

Before the consultative committees were established the brunt of the work was being carried by Citizens' Advice Bureaux and Family Welfare Associations.[60] Also many International Friendship Organizations were established in order to bring about racial harmony at the local level. Nationally two important multi-racial organizations have emerged. In 1962 the Government set up a Commonwealth Immigrants Advisory Council upon whose report a National Committee for Commonwealth Immigrants was set up in 1964. Its functions are 'to promote and co-ordinate voluntary local activities, organize conferences and research and, upon request or on its own initiative, advise the Government on policy'.[61] In contrast to the NCCI whose tasks revolve around the basic aim of integration through welfare work and non-political activities, the other important body, established in 1965, the National Committee against Racial Discrimination (CARD) was formed with explicit political aims, that is 'to expose cases of discrimination and to demand political action to cope with them'.[62]

In considering organized opinion, we must also mention two institutions, besides the governmental bodies and political organizations, with much potential for influencing the way in

67

which minorities are handled. The Church can provide a natural link for minority groups which are Christian; and its attitude to non-Christian groups can, even in the present secularized conditions, influence general attitudes towards such groups. The Trade Unions occupy a powerful position in the all important work situation. The records of these two institutions are in each case an admixture of prejudice and discrimination at the local and more informal level, and tolerant attitudes at the top formal level. To say this is to give a rather simplified picture, but investigators have reported that coloured people have often been unwelcome in many churches.[63] This has led to a religious *apartheid*: 'in 1967 it was estimated that at least 50 per cent of West Indians who were regular churchgoers attended churches run by and mainly or exclusively attended by coloured people'; and Clifford Hill has also drawn our attention to the mushrooming of numerous small West Indian Pentecostal sects since the early 1960s.[64] Yet Church leaders of all denominations have made anti-discriminatory statements[65] and many Churchmen and Church associations have been in the vanguard of the drive towards integration.[66]

The situation regarding non-coloured minorities has been rather similar. To illustrate again from the religious sphere, the anti-Polish campaign was strengthened in some parts of Britain, as for instance in Scotland, by insinuations that the Poles were Papist spies.[67] This was a reminder of the militant Orange Associations which expressed the anti-Irish prejudices in religious terms in Scotland a century before. England was not without its anti-Irish, anti-Catholic militants as Orange Associations in Lancashire and the Gordon riots in London have shown.[68] Neither the prejudices nor the militancy have completely disappeared. To give just two examples, as recently as 1957 the Chairman of the London Sessions remarked that 'This court is infested with Irishmen who come here to commit offences and the more that can be persuaded to go back the better',[69] and in 1959 the Catholic Archbishop of Liverpool was stoned when he visited Irish Catholics lodging in a staunchly Protestant district.[70]

Religious segregation is again seen in the existence of

separate Polish Roman Catholic parishes, with their own clergy and special services, as indeed the Irish Catholics are still often segregated in this sphere. There are also the separate Greek Orthodox Cypriot churches, five of which were established in London between 1948 and 1965.[71] Yet at the same time the need for Christian unity has been espoused by most church leaders. Again as James Parkes shows, much anti-Semitic prejudice is created by many of the Christian clergy. He contends that Judaism and the story of the Jewish people are usually not presented fairly in sermons or at Sunday School.[72] At the same time Christian leaders have played a significant role in the efforts of the Council of Christians and Jews, established in 1942 and functioning through its twenty branches, to foster better relationships between Jews and Christians. The contrast between attitudes at the local level and those of the leading cadres, and even a kind of ambivalence throughout, can be seen equally well in the Trade Union movement. We shall, however, look at this in some detail in Chapter 4.

Finally our attention turns to the small fringe organizations whose express purpose it is to oppose the establishment of minority groups in Britain. The best known pre-war organization was the British Union of Fascists which launched vicious attacks on the Jews in this country in the 1930s, at the time of the ascendancy of Nazism in Germany and Fascism in Italy. The organization was banned at the beginning of the war and its leaders gaoled. It was reconstituted after the war under the name of the Union Movement, but it has faded into insignificance, some of its thunder being acquired by newer neo-Nazi groups such as the National Socialist Movement. The Union Movement appears to have shifted its attack from the Jews to the coloured minorities. Similarly, the British National Party, another extremist group, has slightly modified its view towards Jews, declaring that it does not wish to carry out a 'final solution'; but it has hardened its policy on coloured minorities. The National Socialist Movement on the other hand continued with the avowed intention of 'getting rid of' the Jews and has kept almost exclusively to this aim.[73] More recently, however, the former leader of this movement has entered a by-election with his new organization called the British Movement and has adopted a platform concerned not with Jews but with the repatriation of coloured people.[74]

The activities of these groups fall into two main categories although these can overlap. The use of violence through paramilitary groups as in the pre-war East End or in the swastika daubings and arson against synagogues in 1959 and again in 1965 may demonstrate ulterior political motives. So may the spasmodic dissemination of virulent anti-Semitic literature. At the same time public meetings designed to gain followers often degenerate into affrays. The fringe groups have had some success in gaining publicity through such activities, but they have been regarded mainly as a nuisance and have not had much of an impact on Britain. In their attempts to gain popular support by democratic means they have also had limited success. The British National Party candidate for Southall, with a heavy concentration of coloured immigrants, gained less than one-eighth of the vote and forfeited his deposit in the 1964 General Election. This did, however, represent 3,410 votes, which constituted 9 per cent of the total votes.[75] The fringe political parties often put up candidates in local elections, where special conditions and low polls may be more in their favour. Greater success than that achieved by simply putting up candidates has accrued to racialist organizations which have not entered politics directly by aims to be represented in Parliament and have avoided identification with Fascism or Nazism. As Paul Foot says:

The plain fact is that the Immigration Control Associations which arose in Birmingham and the surrounding area in 1960 and 1961, by means of their concentration on a single issue, their ability to move freely among members of established political parties and their dissociation from nominal Fascism, had a greater impact on British politics than any of the extremist right-wing parties could have done.[76]

It is interesting to speculate on this score whether Mr Enoch Powell and his supporters will decide to further their recent anti-coloured campaign within the Conservative party or opt for the establishment of a new party.

Defence and Protest

The experience of prejudice and discrimination in everyday life by members of minority groups, and their awareness of the existence also of more hostile elements, naturally led to reactions which can be expressed in a variety of ways. Three kinds of responses can be discerned: peaceful withdrawal, defence, and militancy. Examples of the first category are many: there can be no doubt that anti-Semitic prejudices have contributed vastly to Jews keeping to themselves; Zubrzycki states clearly that in the case of the Poles the reaction was a greater determination to uphold their culture and national distinctness, although they did believe that such preservation of a national entity was anyway necessary for keeping up their politically oriented struggle;[77] and A. T. Carey reported that coloured students who found difficulties in being accepted by their white peers have had a tendency to withdraw.[78]

It is true that withdrawal may not be induced only by the prejudices of the dominant group; it may be due to the strangeness of the new environment, particularly to newer immigrants, or to a conscious wish by minority members and especially by its leading members to preserve the cultural values of the group. At the same time the evidence suggests that withdrawal is also a way of responding to prejudice. Simpson and Yinger regard it as an extreme form of avoidance which in some circumstances minority members practise in order to preserve their self-respect and to gain status in their own group, since status is denied to them in the larger community.[79]

The response to prejudice and discrimination may, however, take the form of defence and protest, and the protest may become militant. The defence or the protest may be carried out by individuals, in their capacities as members of organizations such as Trade Unions or through other channels such as are provided by the mass media. More often, however, these tasks are carried out by organizations specifically created for such purposes or with multiple purposes, one of which will be that of defence. The West Indian Association in Lancashire was established 'to safeguard the interest of West Indians in the community.'[80] The Oi T'ung Association, the oldest Chinese association in London, was formed to fulfil two main objects: 'to protect its members from discrimination by the host society and to provide members with mutual aid'.[81] The Board of Deputies of British Jews acts in a general sense as a representative body, but it also carries out the specific task of defence through a committee created for that purpose.[82] In the case of the World Jewish Congress one of the objects is clearly 'to secure the rights, status and interests of Jews and Jewish communities and to defend them wherever they are denied, violated or imperilled'.[83] The Association of Jewish Ex-Service Men has on the other hand primarily an interest in defence, and its membership and activities fluctuate with the incidence of anti-Semitism.[84]

The examples of bodies formed by minorities to combat discrimination could be multiplied manifold. One could add to the list the Indian Workers' Association,[85] the Polish Ex-Combatants' Association, the Irish Self Determination League, the Connolly Association, and so on. The National Committee against Racial Discrimination is another such organization. Mary Grigg, reporting on one of their meetings organized for general public discussion, discerned how coloured minorities can feel powerless and rejected in a democratic society.[86] It can be easily shown how such rejection of any minority group leads to withdrawal, protest and ultimately militancy. The experiences of the Jews, the Irish, and the coloured minorities have all illustrated this trend. The 'ghettoization' of the Jewish immigrants at the end of the last century soon bred a protest movement. As Lloyd Gartner puts it:

The efflorescence of the Jewish labour and socialist movement, fully equipped with a comprehensive ideological basis, was in some ways the outcome of the immigrants' sense of deprivation of the benefits which were expected of life in a new country. On the other hand, it also represents the first response of Jewish thought to an industrial and urban environment, influenced by nineteenth century European socialism.[87]

The Jewish immigrant worker, therefore, joined Jewish Socialist societies and Trade Unions and was being influenced by the *Polish Yidel*, a Socialist newspaper. Revolutionary

Socialist and anarchist societies also developed and their mouthpiece the *Arbeiter Freind* (Worker's Friend) declared: 'In order to spread true socialism among Jewish workers . . . We wish in a word, to change entirely the present order of tyranny and injustice . . . it must . . . give way to a new and just society . . .'[88] The militants ridiculed and clashed even physically with those adhering to the traditional outlook of the minority. However, they were themselves rejected by some of the English Socialists: the early English Marxists, for instance, were regarded on the whole as anti-Semitic.[89] The Jewish Socialist was in fact forced to operate in his own *milieu*, a situation which, looked at from the ideological angle, was a contradiction in terms. It was perhaps due to this that Socialism was replaced by Socialist-Zionism in the early part of this century. In 1905 the Leeds *Poale Zion* (Workers of Zion) adopted the following platform: '(A) To create a national-political centre in Palestine for the Jewish people. (B) To lead a struggle for civil and national rights in the Diaspora. (C) To struggle against the present economic order equally with other proletarian organizations.'[90]

The story of the Irish worker in England is not very different from that of the Jews. The Irish were active in Trade Union organization in the second half of the nineteenth century as they were in the earlier Chartist movement. But the Irish, as the Jews, were active in their own *milieu* – the Dock Strike of 1889 was on the whole an Irish affair as the majority of dock workers and leaders were Irish. There was in fact some animosity between English and Irish workers and their fight for workers' interests often ran on separate lines. Thus, although the Irish worker initially entertained ideas of changing society radically and was animated by Socialist ideas, this soon gave way to a powerful preoccupation with the further-ance of Irish independence and nationalism. As early as 1886 a failure to get through a Home Rule Bill for Ireland produced protest demonstrations throughout the country. The policy of the United Irish League was 'that the Irish vote should not be committed to any British party but directed wherever the interests of Ireland demanded such action.'[91] By the turn of the century, Irish clubs, literary societies and publications

73

provided manifestations of withdrawal, and a nationalist stance was quite clearly established. Developments in the early part of this century led from withdrawal and protest to militancy, a phenomenon which lingered on for years. The quest for Irish Home Rule and the disastrous struggles in Ireland in the 1920s between Irish Nationalists and British forces, led to an extension of the violence to British cities. Cells of the Irish Republican Army became active in Liverpool, Manchester, Newcastle, Glasgow and London – warehouses were burnt down and windows broken; Irish activists were gaoled and London crowds attacked their sympathisers.[92] As John Jackson says:

The establishment of the Irish Free State, later to become the Irish Republic did little to change the allegiance of the immigrant to Ireland's cause. The rancour that had surrounded the struggle and its unsatisfactory resolution in the partition of Ireland was crystallized in a new nationalistic loyalty to Ireland. The exile status of the immigrant was enhanced by the development of the new nation and his homeland and its cause was continued in the struggle for a United Ireland.[93]

The coloured minorities have also exhibited changes from a peaceful defensive posture to one of militant reaction. The early immigrants were content with ameliorating their position by mutual aid and were concerned with controlling elements which might, through their attitudes, bring disrepute to the minority. The Coloured Peoples' Mutual Aid Society and the Stepney Coloured Peoples' Association played such roles. On occasion the coloured immigrant would react violently to attacks on him, as he did after the minor clashes of 1958 in Nottingham and Notting Hill. So did the Irish in the 1920s and the Jews before the Second World War. But such incidents do not reflect the real change: the trend among the more recent arrivals. To quote Judith Henderson: 'They reject the subservient role which the white community expects them to play, and they reject equally the restraints placed on them by their own people'.[94] Undoubtedly there has been a diffusion of ideas on which the new militants rely. The Racial Adjustment Action Society, with branches in many of Britain's cities, was directly influenced by the Black Muslims from America.[95] The Black Power movement itself was influenced it appears, according to its early leader William du Bois, by Jewish nationalism. Du Bois wrote: 'The African movement means to us what the Zionist movement must mean to the Jews.'[96] But whatever the ideological borrowings might have been, the scene in Britain, according to A. Sivanandan, has changed in the past decade from one which affords the opportunity to solve racial problems by the peaceful efforts of both white and coloured liberals to one which is quickly becoming ripe for action by black militants.[97] The motto of these people is 'to fight back' and the Socialist or anarchist element in the expected fight is not lacking. This is evident from publications such as the *Black Dwarf*, established in its present format in 1968, and the fact that RAAS are looking to industrial action as a major weapon.[98] Militant action against discrimination was pledged at the launching of the Black People's Alliance in 1968. To this twenty out of the more than one thousand immigrant organizations in the country were invited, representing West Indians, Africans, Indians and Pakitanis.[99] The militants appear to be gaining ground in immigrant organizations, such as the Indian Workers' Association. And actual violence also broke out at a Black Power demonstration in London in April 1970.[100]

As in the case of the Jews and the Irish, the native English Trade Unionist or Socialist is not fighting for the minority group – in this case the coloured group – he even tends to be antagonistic towards it.[101] It is not surprising, therefore, to find coloured workers interested in forcing justice to be done without outside help, if necessary by looking inward to nationalism – that is by establishing 'a self-sufficient, autonomous, and as it were, a regional society divided from white society', and by seeking 'to rise in the world without giving up what is distinctively *black*'. These are, according to Philip Mason, the aims of Black Power,[102] and as such do not differ much from the reactions of other minorities in Britain to prejudice and discrimination.

Legislative Measures

As we have seen above it would be a mistake to think that legislation to control immigration is a completely new phenomenon. Aliens' Acts have been passed intermittently for the last hundred years and certain regulations regarding the entry of immigrants and their settlement have existed for hundreds of years.[103] The groups so controlled included French Huguenots, East European Jews, and Christians from various parts of Europe, as well as Africans and Asians. As for measures to control discrimination against immigrants or members of minority groups, reliance has been placed on the whole on English common law upholding basic rights for all citizens, irrespective of the colour of their skin as Lord Justice Salmon's pronouncement illustrated in 1958. On the positive side in matters of religion, however, the Jewish minority has received special consideration by provisions in enactment at times going back into the last century, and concerned with such matters as marriage registrations, the observance of the Sabbath where this clashes with civic duties, and facilities for the observance of Jewish dietary laws.

Despite these precedents there is a new element in the legislative measures taken in the 1960s. The newness shows itself firstly in that the fresh enactments attempt to control the entry of *British citizens* who are coloured; and secondly in the direct but rather ineffective attempt to counteract some forms of discriminatory practice. The position at present is, therefore, that the entry of immigrants into the United Kingdom is regulated by four different types of control. First, citizens of Eire, although non-British, are in practice uncontrolled. Second, the entry of *aliens*, that is foreigners who come from non-Commonwealth countries, is controlled by the 1919 Aliens Act amended by the 1953 Aliens Order. For this category there is no ceiling fixed on numbers coming to work here and dependants enter at the discretion of the authorities. Third, there are the Commonwealth and UK Citizens who hold passports issued by colonial governments. Their entry is controlled by the 1962 and 1968 Commonwealth Immigrants Acts and the 1965 White Paper on Commonwealth Immigration which put a ceiling of 8,500 workers holding vouchers, that is coming to a job, being allowed in per year, with the right of wives to join husbands and children under sixteen to join parents. Finally, there are the non-resident UK citizens with passports issued by UK Government. Entry for people in this category is controlled by the 1968 Act and it applies to such UK citizens who have no 'substantial connexion' with the UK, the maximum number allowed in yearly being 1,500, with provisions similar to those in the previous category.[104]

What emerges from the different rules applied to foreigners desiring to enter Britain is that whilst citizens from the Republic of Ireland are free to enter and are subject to no restrictions, and whilst other aliens are restricted but without a specified quota being applied to them, those who hold British passports, on account of their citizenship of Commonwealth countries, are rigorously controlled. This is not as paradoxical as it appears. There is a very long tradition of free movement between Ireland and England which has remained unaffected by the creation of Eire. Aliens from other countries, say from Europe or the United States, are not seeking to settle in this country in large numbers. In contrast, Commonwealth immigrants in increasing numbers were seeking opportunities for work and trade in the 1950s and 1960s. It is true that anticipation of the passing of the Control Acts has had the effect of accelerating the rush, as noted above. A special case in point would be the Sikhs, whose sojourn in England was often temporary as they were able to rely on the 'joint family' structure to look after their wives and children in India for the period they were working in Britain, but who, with the imminence of the Control Acts, began to bring over their entire families and settle permanently in Britain.[105] Another instance is the Indian minority in Kenya, many of whose members who might otherwise not have done so who feared the ill-effects of Kenyanization rushed to Britain early in 1968 to beat the ban.[106] Whichever way the causal relationship between immigration and control is seen and interpreted, the fact that now stands out is that a most rigorous control is being applied to people who happen to be coloured. Another aftermath or side-effect of the Control Acts has been to debase the value of a British

77

passport. Thus holders of such passports, if Kenya Asians for instance, have for all practical purposes become stateless persons unable to enjoy citizenship rights anywhere.[107]

The last points may suggest discrimination exercised at the highest level, and it is hardly possible to explain the instituted measures purely in pragmatic terms. But both the Labour Government responsible for tightening the controls and the Conservative Party who often appear even tougher, are in substantial agreement that those who are already in Britain must be treated on the basis of equality and full citizenship rights. To facilitate this, in view of mounting evidence of discrimination practised against coloured citizens in particular and other minority groups in general, the Labour Government passed the Race Relations Acts of 1965 and 1968. These include measures to deal with discrimination on grounds of colour, race, ethnic or national origins in the fields of employment, housing, public services, the provision of goods and services generally and such other facilities as education and banking. Incitement to racial hatred has also been made unlawful. 'Discrimination' has been legally defined as differential treatment, and 'incitement to racial hatred' is regarded by the law as an act having the intent of stirring up hatred against sections of the public distinguished by the criteria of colour, race, ethnicity or nationality, by means of (a) the publication or distribution of written matter which is threatening, abusive or insulting; or (b) the use in any public place or at a public meeting of words which are threatening, abusive or insulting. Whilst with 'discrimination' offences the proceedings are civil and are preceded by attempts at conciliation carried out by special committees of the Race Relations Board, the proceedings in the case of the 'incitement to racial hatred' are criminal and carry stiff penalties, including substantial fines and imprisonment.[108] Although prosecution for incitement can be instituted in England and Wales only by the Attorney-General, the Race Relations Board is on the whole charged with securing compliance with the Acts. In addition the Community Relations Commission has been established by the 1968 Act with 'the positive role of encouraging harmonious relations between the different ethnic groups within the community'.[109]

It is too early to ask how effective these measures have proved. But we can examine some indications as to the likely effectiveness of the Acts and ponder on the views aired about the anti-discrimination legislation. Considering simply the increase in the number of complaints received, the wider scope of the 1968 Act is immediately revealed although the overall patterns created by the 1965 Act remained; namely, most of the complaints were about employment and housing. The Race Relations Board stresses, however, that its effectiveness is not to be judged merely by the number of complaints received or dealt with. 'The settlement of one complaint', they say, 'can change the policy of a whole industry'. Furthermore, the value of the Acts, according to the Board, lies in their 'declaratory effect', bringing about non-discriminatory policies in many major firms.[110] The Board recognizes, however, that declarations and intents must be backed up by action. The Board undertakes such action in the first instance through its conciliation machinery. In the Fforde Greene Affair, where an attempt was made at a Leeds pub to impose a colour bar, the conciliation committee showed its ability to act speedily, but one commentator discerned in that case a lack of confidence in the Board evidenced by the fact that the complainants contacted in the first place a local voluntary association, and he thought this pointed to the need for strengthening the liaison work between voluntary groups and the Board.[111]

However, the more direct criticism of the Race Relations Act concerns its basic weakness, due to the Board's not having the right to subpoena witnesses or to inspect documents. Finally some disagree with the denial to the individual of the right to take action himself if he is dissatisfied with the steps taken on his behalf by the Race Relations Board.[112]

The functioning of the Community Relations Commission is even more difficult to assess because of the recentness of its creation. The Commission took over from the National Committee of Commonwealth Immigrants in 1968. Unlike the latter, which was a voluntary body, the Commission is statutory and subsidized by the Government. Its enhanced position in financial and status terms has not prevented the raising of many problems. Bureaucratization appears to have led to dissatisfaction among some of its officials. A number of resignations have taken place among field workers, who have decided to form a staff association despite reports of opposition by some of their superiors.[113] The main problem seems to be, however, that the Commission and particularly some of its officers have found their position awkward in view of the Janus-faced policy of the Government: enjoining the Commission to promote racial harmony and at the same time employing stringent and sometimes unfair measures against would-be immigrants. One Liaison Officer explained that she resigned because she found she was 'in a false position over accepting a salary from Government grant-aid in order to improve community relations to which the Commonwealth Immigrants Act did appalling damage'.[114] And the Chairman of the Commission has himself complained about the Home Office's failure to adequately consult the Commission as laid down under the 1968 Act, thus hindering the improvement of community relations.[115]

The question of the effectiveness of legislative measures can be raised on many sides. Have the Control Acts still left loopholes through which immigrants who are the relatives of those already here can gain entry?[116] Can legislation really change the attitudes of local authority officers who may in their interpretation of the law and its application appear to the minorities concerned as evincing prejudiced behaviour? Timidity in the town hall has certainly worked against the improvement of the living conditions of new immigrants and so has often the tacit agreement between house-agent and house-seller in the 'better districts'. And how can the legislative machinery do away with the unconscious influences that stereotyped beliefs have on the very people who are called upon to implement the law of the land. Thus, Bob Hepple maintains that 'there is evidence that in the early years of coloured immigration some lay magistrates made disparaging remarks about immigrants, in much the same way as severe sentences for assault are sometimes imposed on Irishmen on the grounds that they are by habit unsober and prone to brawling'.[117]

Finally, the effectiveness of legislation may also be judged by both omissions and inclusions. As an example of an omission there is what for the Jews can be regarded as the vexed question of not including 'religion' among the criteria of unlawful discrimination or hate propaganda.[118] On the other hand there is the recommendation of the recent comprehensive race relations report that the section of the law dealing with incitement to racial hatred by speech or in writing should be repealed.[119] The arguments for jettisoning the law revolve around the question of freedom of speech, sympathy aroused for those prosecuted, and the unwanted publicity of objectionable utterances to which prosecution gives rise. To this it may be retorted that libel laws also come near to the question of freedom of speech, that there is no real evidence that sympathy would be gained by those prosecuted for inciting racial hatred, and that publicity is double-edged.[120] It is of course true that legislation alone will not do. Voluntary effort and a basic re-education and re-orientation in one's views of different segments of society are absolute necessities. The law cannot be sustained without a good deal of 'moral' support. This is not to argue that legislation is not useful or powerful. It can alter the size of minority groups as it has done in the past and continues to do now; and it can strongly influence the atmosphere in which the minorities have to live. But ultimately the prevalent social environment will depend, particularly in its subtler nuances, on the prejudices and foibles of the majority.

Why Prejudice?

Most of the definitions of prejudice emanate from psychological studies or theories which are invariably concerned with the mechanisms at work where an individual's behaviour evinces prejudices against other individuals belonging to some group. Gordon Allport's is such a definition: 'an avertive or hostile attitude towards a person who belongs to a group, simply because he belongs to that group, and is therefore presumed to have the objectionable qualities ascribed to that group'.[121] At the cognitive level the main elements then stressed by psychologists are: *uncritical generalization or stereotyping*, that is attributing to all group members qualities observed in a few of them; *selective emphasis*, that is emphasizing qualities which appertain not only to the group held in prejudice; *omission*, a tendency to overlook desirable qualities; and *inconsistent value judgements*, where similar acts or characteristics are condemned when committed by one group, but condoned or even praised when committed by another. Other factors building up prejudices are reliance on hearsay, suggestibility, self-deception, rationalization, etc.[122]

At the theoretical level we have had two main kinds of explanation from the psychologists. There is the Frustration-Aggression theory, which revolves around the scapegoat idea: since the agent of frustration is often too powerful, the individual will resort to *displaced aggression* rather than *direct aggression*, and this explains why hostility is shown towards groups for no apparent reason. There is a joke about a conversation between a Jew and a Nazi. Nazi: 'The Jews are responsible for all the evil in the world.' Jew: 'No, not the Jews, the cyclists.' Nazi: 'Why the cyclists?' Jew: 'Why the Jews?' Groups will, therefore, even be invented, but at all events their important characteristic will be that they are unable to hit back. An offshoot of this theory is the postulation of the *Authoritarian Personality* profile, identified by a cluster of high prejudice, and closely related to this is the *projection theory*, according to which the prejudiced person accuses minorities of motives he himself has, but which he fears and is guilty about. This leads basically to the Freudian notion that prejudice is 'an irrational, pathological phenomenon arising from the individual's own inadequacies'.[123]

This kind of theory was well received since it blamed prejudice and hostility on disturbed individuals and, therefore, did not require an examination of the social system in search of factors that might produce conflict and prejudiced behaviour. But it did not square with the empirical evidence. Prejudice and scapegoatism were not practised only by a few maladjusted individuals. Given certain circumstances, by and large, whole groups and societies can come to hold prejudiced views and the group as a whole or its members individually will act according to those views. This applies not only to Nazi Germany but also to other societies, whilst our own material in this chapter shows that time and again the appearance of ethnic minorities on the British scene, whether it was the Irish, the Jews, coloured groups or groups from Europe, has produced similar reactions in the native population: namely, widespread prejudice and some outright hostility when given a lead, especially in some circumstances such as hard economic conditions, followed by legislation to limit numbers and much discussion on how to solve the problems claimed to have been created by the existence of such groups. The evidence suggests that there is something in the social situation which gives rise to this recurring pattern. It surely is not simply a matter of a few maladjusted individuals, however much such people are bound to aggravate the situation particularly in some of its manifestations.

To meet this kind of empirical reasoning social-psychologists have provided us with the second major explanatory scheme. This states that individuals have a need to conform to, to identify with, and to be integrated into a social group. In this identification process, starting with child socialization, they tend to dichotomize social groups, emphasizing on the one hand their loyalty, solidarity, etc., to their 'in-group', and on the other hand exaggerating their distance from and disagreement with the 'out-group'. Since ethnic minorities, whatever their distinguishing marks, readily form such 'out-groups' they become easy targets for prejudice.[124] A less sophisticated theory puts forward the idea of a fear of, or hostility to, strangers, which ethologists have simply traced to animal behaviour. They explain xenophobia by stating that 'since most species divide up any given area into group territories, frontiers are created which are jealously guarded'[125] and that struggles then ensue to exclude extra-territorial members. This is necessary, it is said, for survival, hence the hostility shown towards intruders who are also seen as competitors. It may be noted, however, that those who have traced aggressive behaviour, manifested in prejudice and hostility, to instincts or drives have been criticized on the ground that there is a good deal of evidence that such behaviour is learned.[126]

The trouble with such an explanation is that prejudices are not always directed only against strangers. Social classes and religious groups are often similarly prejudiced towards each other and are in conflict. Furthermore, in some situations strangers are in fact positively welcomed as was the case with the Hungarian and Czech refugees. Nevertheless, 'in-group'-'out-group' alignments are factually observable social phenomena. In our final conclusions we shall attempt to analyse the specific situations in which 'in-group'-'out-group' hostilities will manifest themselves. The sociological analysis of the deeper causes of ethnic group hostility and prejudice arising out of particular social situations is, therefore, worth exploring here briefly.

Sociologists draw our attention to the social situation created by the increasing heterogeneity of societies which has come about through conquest and empire building, the rise of nation-states, and greater population movements possible in industrial society,[127] a point stressed in the first chapter. Such situations have thrown up groups of people with distinctive cultures or physical characteristics placed side by side, some finding themselves by virtue of the new social situation in an inferior position. One of the best examples of this, analysed by John Rex, is the colonial situation, more recently imported into metropolitan Britain.[128] Here the ex-colonials are treated as an external proletariat, regarded as fit only for some menial tasks and relegated to the bottom of the social scale. Prejudices here are usually manifested in the unequal distribution of material goods, prestige and power.

Two important questions remain. First, is this situation not simply a special case of the stratification system which obtains in our society? Second, are the patterns of prejudice shown towards the various minorities in Britain explicable in these sociological or social situation terms? The question of the identity between 'minority situation' and 'class situation' is a complex one.[129] It is true that examples can be drawn not only from the situation of the coloured ex-colonials to show that minorities fitted or were made to fit into the low-class positions of the stratification order. The Irish in Britain, the East European Jews and to some extent the Cypriots have found themselves in similar situations. Furthermore, prejudices were used to maintain the situation and justify it, although some, particularly the Jews, were able to break out of that situation despite the obstacles. The earlier Jewish immigrants in the years prior to the East European influx were not in the exploited proletariat position, but occupied as merchants and pedlars a marginal position, and the same applies to most of the Sikhs who have come to Britain more recently. There are exceptions, however, to this overall pattern. The Poles were able to bring with them the whole socio-economic structure of their original home. True, some of them, as often happens among *émigrés*, have become *déclassé*, but they could not be regarded as falling on the whole into a marginal situation or being a purely bottom of the scale exploited proletariat at any time since the inception of the community.

But we are not dealing here simply with the question of how general is the phenomenon of the relegation of minorities to low-class positions. The question is whether from the analysis of such a situation we can arrive at an adequate explanation of the existence of prejudices. What this line of reasoning suggests is that the economic relations between minority and majority groups demonstrate the wish by the latter, principally the ruling section of it, to dominate, and that this goal is being achieved by means of prejudice, discrimination and exploitation.[130] This then is not basically different from class exploitation. But in effect there are areas other than the economic where the majority appears to wish to dominate. Religious prejudices *vis-à-vis* the Jews and the Irish, and nationalistic ones as those against the Italians and Poles are particularly good examples here. We must arrive, therefore, at a more general understanding of the processes involved in what social scientists have called *culture-contact*.[131] As John Rex brings out in his analysis of some of the writings on this topic, this situation, where several ethnically distinct groups come to live in close proximity with each other, creates a pluralistic social framework in which these groups of differing cultures are essentially in conflict.[132]

For the explanation of this conflict one must revert to the idea of 'in-group'-'out-group' awareness, mentioned earlier. The essential point here is that 'in-group'-'out-group' hostilities are less likely to develop in homogeneous societies. It is also true, as the evidence suggests from the study both of the dynamics of social stratification and of minority-majority relation, that such hostilities are much more likely to appear where material problems are at hand. Prejudices against minorities have flourished more often in times of economic crisis, and are more widespread in areas where the minority is seen to compete for housing and employment. The evidence for the latter is anticipated here and will be found in the next chapter.

The overall picture then is that there are two basic elements at work in the causation of prejudice. There is the heterogeneity of a society which accentuates 'in-group'-'out-group' differences and thus heightens ethnocentrism, and there is the economic relation between weaker 'inferior' groups on the one hand and the stronger dominant group on the other, which provides the most important arena for competition, exploitation and conflict. Ethnocentrism is not to be interpreted as a mystical fear of some physical characteristic of strangers. It is simply that culture contact may result in an exaggeratedly favourable evaluation of the group's own system and a deprecation of the newly encountered culture or system. This in a sense 'legitimizes' the conflict which is more likely to arise where economic relationships are concerned. It may also shift attention from the class differences in the majority society. The attempt to dominate will then be made on behalf of or by the majority as a whole, and thus ethnic minorities will experience widespread prejudice held against them. The danger in such a situation is not only that if the process is unabated it will have injurious effects on minorities; it lies also in its developing into the sort of conflict which could destroy the whole social fabric, as recent events in the United States have indicated.

In Chapter 4 we shall examine in some detail the conditions of minorities in Britain as seen in the main urban-industrial areas, and then go on to conclusions about the overall trend in minority-majority relations.

4 The Urban Maelstrom

Large-scale minority settlement in Britain is a phenomenon of industrial society, and the process of settlement has been unfolded chiefly in the context of urban life and its complexities. It is true that 'A job and a roof over his head . . . are the main immediate needs of the newcomer'[1] but these are not simple matters; they stand in relationship to a multiplicity of other factors and they influence one another. The newcomer's background including his skill and education, the cultural diversities of different groups, the socio-economic situation in the receiving country, the system of stratification and wealth allocation, the attitudes and ideologies prevailing both within the country and internationally, the new situations created by minority-majority relations, all are factors that will shape the lives not only of the newcomers but of all citizens of the urban centres.

The task of describing, let alone analysing, in detail the mass of facts[2] and the intricate inter-relationships between the various facets of urban life may appear too daunting. However, by using a sociological framework, of the kind developed by John Rex, it is possible to throw light on the major determinants of minority-majority relations. Rex emphasizes the need to see clearly the basic social system distinctive of the Western industrial city.[3] I shall use that framework to analyse the housing and employment situations, and I shall also attempt to use what comparative evidence there is on social and ecological mobility as an index of the respective positions of minority groups and the indigenous population in the overall urban system.

Housing

As a rule new immigrants have to put up with housing inferior both qualitatively and quantitatively. One criterion for the latter situation is the number of rooms occupied by each household. Information on this is provided by the Race Relations Report using data from the 1966 Census. The figures refer to London and the West Midlands and show wide differences. In selected London boroughs the average number of rooms per English household was 4.29. The figures for immigrant households were: coloured 2.93, Cypriots 3.58, Irish 2.72. When this is set against the number of persons per household – English 2.66, coloured 3.47, Cypriots, 3.38, Irish 3.17 – the higher density per room amongst immigrants becomes immediately evident.[4]

Density of occupation per room has been established in fact as 'the most useful single diagnostic of housing conditions'.[5] For coloured immigrants there is a much higher density than for the English. In the London conurbation the former had a density of 1.05 in 1955 compared with 0·57 for the latter.[6] Both the evidence from the 1966 Census and that analysed by R. B. Davison from the 1961 Census show unmistakably that the West Indians have the highest densities. The Indians and Pakistanis seem less badly housed; so do the Cypriots and Irish. The Poles have achieved a position similar to that of the English in this respect.[7]

Another criterion that in fact links the qualitative and quantitative aspects of housing is the sharing of households. Shared households imply a high density, but even more they signify the lack of exclusive use of household facilities and raise the problem of privacy. These are factors which obviously have a serious effect on the quality of life. The evidence once again shows the immigrants, and particularly the newer coloured groups, to be worse off than the English. Housing tenure too is indicative of the positions of different groups. The most significant difference is in the necessity for coloured immigrants to rely heavily on renting furnished accommodation, involving them in greater expense and less security, as against the minimal use of such accommodation by the English. In the London conurbation 43.6 per cent of coloured immigrants rented furnished accommodation but only 2.6 per cent of the English did so. In the West Midlands conurbation the figures were 21.4 per cent and 1.3 per cent respectively. On the other hand very few of the coloured immigrants rent accommodation from local authorities, 4.2 per cent against 22.2 per cent of the English in London and 8.2 per cent against 39.1 per cent in the West Midlands.[8]

There is yet another aspect indicating 'problem housing' which is reflected by the inspections and prosecutions carried out by the Public Health Department. The figures given below also reveal that immigrants are not all at the receiving end of inferior housing; many of the bad landlords come from their own ranks. The authors whose table we reproduce say, however, that some of the problems leading to prosecutions arise out of misunderstandings between immigrant landlords and Public Health Inspectors.

TABLE 4.1: *Inspections of Houses and Prosecutions arising*

Birmingham: 8 June 1962–8 February 1964[9]

Owners	Houses inspected		Ill-managed houses	Houses lacking facilities	Over occup-ation	Summonses issued	
	No.	%	%	%	%	No.	%
Pakistanis	658	42	61	75	83	530	70
Indians	292	19	56	71	83	210	27
Others	611	39	5	8	9	16	3
TOTAL	1,561	100	—	—	—	756	100

The question that has to be faced now is how the problem conditions of overcrowding in sub-standard housing have arisen. Before giving the answer, which will be found to contain many causal elements, it must be stated that housing problems leading in extreme form to the industrial 'slum' have not been connected solely with the existence of immigrant minorities. The inadequate housing provided for workers by the 'captains of industry', and the ravages of the Second

89

World War have led to both the shortage and the inferior quality of housing in the older industrial sectors of cities.[10] It is true, however, that large-scale immigration in the post-war period has aggravated the situation, as did also the natural increase of the indigenous population.

But the new problems have arisen in the 'zone of transition' in the decaying older suburbs where the upper-middle classes have formerly lived (see Ch. 2, p. 43 above). These are the areas which have provided the first stage accommodation for many minorities, by means of boarding-houses and rooming-houses. Sheila Patterson describes how the process worked in one such area in South London:

The district contained many large short-lease Victorian houses, most of them dilapidated, some recently derequisitioned and containing statutory tenants paying uneconomic pre-war rentals. This type of property had ceased to be attractive to English house-purchasers, to property investors, and even to speculators. As a consequence, many leaseholders were willing to sell before the leases ran out and they became liable for large dilapidation payments – to sell at any price to any bidder, Irish, Polish, Cypriot or coloured.[11]

Often however, as the Milner Holland Report has pointed out, even for sub-standard houses immigrants have had to pay prices far above their market value.

To make such house purchases economically viable the new immigrant landlords had to institute the multi-occupation of their properties. As building societies would not advance mortgages on such properties, the immigrant either spent his capital savings or borrowed at very high interest rates, which meant that only multi-occupation and spending the absolute minimum on properties which were already in disrepair could possibly keep him solvent. But there was no problem of would-be tenants. The discrimination rampant on the housing market, mentioned in Chapter 3,[12] and the special rules of local authorities leading to differential allocation of public housing, have provided the masses of immigrants who were prepared to pay the high rents for low-grade accommodation. These landlords were in fact providing a service which was of a very low grade although not always through their own fault. A by-product of this was, however, 'Rachmanism' which refers to unscrupulous speculators manipulating inter-racial tensions to replace low-rent tenants with more profitable ones.[13] But some decaying parts of urban centres have always bred crime and immorality and it is important to distinguish the purveyors of this kind of 'twilight zone' business from most immigrant landlords who often as owner-occupiers sub-let many of their large properties, sometimes at lower than reasonable rents, to fellow immigrants from their original countries, but who make up for this by charging exorbitant rents to those of other ethnic groups.[14]

Despite the passing of Race Relations Acts, discrimination in housing, particularly against coloured immigrants, has continued. Whilst the Chairman of the Race Relations Board has claimed that the deeply insulting and provocative advertisements saying 'No coloureds' have virtually disappeared,[15] more subtle discrimination of the kind tested by the PEP survey is likely to be continuing. The Board itself has lost on technical grounds its first case against a Yorkshire building firm which refused to sell a home to a coloured man because it was against company policy 'for business reasons'.[16] Again the Board has indicted Wolverhampton Corporation of unlawfulness in stipulating that people born outside Britain must wait two years before qualifying for a council home compared with one year for the native population, and has condemned it for publishing this policy.[17] The Cullingworth Report has proposed that local councils should keep records of housing needs among immigrants so that inadvertent discrimination should be avoided, and that where necessary the Government should look into the housing policies of some local authorities where these result in discrimination.[18] The fact remains that the local authorities and their officers wield much power in regard to housing which so far has not been used even-handedly. In addition many authorities have been reluctant to become involved in the problems of the twilight zone, leaving large numbers to manage as best they can in the squalor of the multi-occupied tenements controlled by 'market forces'.[19]

Discrimination has not been the only cause of bad housing and social problems among immigrants. The larger families and particularly the traditional hospitality to newly arrived relatives, giving rise to extended families, have certainly contributed a great deal to over-crowding. This has been true both of more recent minorities, such as the Indians and Pakitanis, and of older established groups such as the Irish and the Jews. The latter experienced particularly difficult conditions in the first decades of their settlement, not unlike those described above relating to the more recently settled minorities. The Jewish quarter in the East End of London suffered a reduction in its housing stock, reduced at the turn of the century to make room for railway facilities and street improvements, at a time when Jewish immigration intensified. Hardly any provision was made for the displaced inhabitants who were joined by their relatives and friends from abroad.

Whitechapel's 8,264 houses of 1871 were only 5,735 in 1901, but the population pent-up in the district rose from 75,552 to 78,768 in the same period, or from an average of 9.14 residents per house in 1871 to 13.74 in 1901. In the latter year, Limehouse, whose housing bore an evil enough reputation, had an average of but 7.97 per house. The crowding reached its greatest extremes in the centre of the Jewish area, where it was claimed that the average density in Whitechapel of 286 per acre reached 600.[20]

This housing shortage described by Lloyd Gartner was reflected at the beginning of the century in the abuse of 'key money' without which accommodation could hardly be rented in the Jewish quarter. The situation was similar in other Jewish urban centres, a good example being the Leylands Jewish ghetto of the same period.[21]

One could reproduce similar pictures for many other earlier immigrant groups. The Irish Rookery in the environs of Tottenham Court Road in the West End of London was notorious for its misery and squalor. In a very small area some 6,000 adults and perhaps nearly 4,000 children were living in insanitary housing at the beginning of the nineteenth century. The conditions were just as bad in the Irish districts of Manchester and Liverpool, where large families lived in damp cellars. Relatively high rents were being paid for single rooms, in which it was not unknown for beds to be sub-let for parts of the day. The Irish middlemen of those days, like the immigrant landlords of today, were providing some kind of service by making miserably inadequate accommodation available for their newly arrived countrymen.[22]

The dockland areas of Cardiff, Liverpool, South Shields and Limehouse in London have all housed numerous small immigrant groups in overcrowded, shabby and unhygienic conditions. Africans, Arabs, Chinese, Malays, Maltese, Somalis and many of other ethnic extractions have experienced these conditions, perhaps the best such surviving polyglot slum being Bute Town in Cardiff.[23]

We must now distinguish two trends in minority housing and settlement which often appear to go hand in hand: congestion and segregation. The account so far has been mainly concerned with explaining how the congestion developed, although the factors of prejudice and discrimination have played powerful roles in producing segregation as well as congestion. Many an urban residence pattern displays well-established boundaries between the minority and indigenous populations. As the newcomers move in, so the older established people move out. With little alternative accommodation the non-minority areas are then jealously guarded, although the demarcation lines do become blurred at times, particularly where older established minorities are concerned. Segregation of minorities is not, however, entirely an imposed one. The voluntary aspect may be as strong if not stronger. The newcomer feels more secure in his own quarter, and may wish, in a positive manner, to maintain his home environment and culture. For this the extreme form of segregated living, the 'ghetto', will prove a very powerful cohesive and preserving force.[24]

But segregation, cohesiveness, congestion and sub-standard housing do not run only along ethnic lines, but also along socio-economic class lines, and we have already indicated how working-class slums were created in the industrial cities of Britain. As John Rex argues, there appear to be two cross-cutting currents in the residential pattern of the industrial city.

His theoretical framework will enable us to see this pattern more clearly. Rex suggests that 'the basic process underlying urban social interaction is competition for scarce and desired types of housing. In this process people are distinguished from one another by their strength in the housing market or, more generally, in the system of housing allocations'.[25] He then develops the idea that because people are differentially placed in this system it is possible to discern the following 'housing classes' in our industrial cities:

1. The outright owners of large houses in desirable areas.
2. Mortgage payers who 'own' whole houses in desirable areas.
3. Council tenants in Council-built houses.
4. Council tenants in slum houses awaiting demolition.
5. Tenants of private house-owners, usually in the inner ring.
6. House owners who must take lodgers to meet loan repayments.
7. Lodgers in rooms.[26]

We shall again take up the theme of the 'housing classes' in the concluding section dealing with the place of minorities in urban development and change. Here it will suffice to point out that ethnicity sharpens the competition and conflict between some groups, such as that between English council tenants in slum houses and immigrants in lodging-houses; and that it blurs the opposing interests of other groups such as immigrant lodging-house proprietors and their tenants if these latter belong to the same ethnic group as the former. It is also worth relating here the 'housing classes' to the diagrammatic presentation of settlement patterns offered in Chapter 2 (above, p. 43). It will be readily seen that Classes 1 and 2 will be found mainly in Zone IV; Class 3 in Zones II and V; Classes 4 and 5 in Zone II; and Classes 6 and 7 in Zone III – the 'zone of transition' where the bulk of the recent immigrants, particularly of the newer minority groups, reside.

Employment

Stereotyped views are often held regarding the types of work in which minority group members are engaged. The Irish are usually regarded as navvies and are said to be primarily connected with the building industry; the Jews as

94

traders and middlemen; the coloured as unskilled labourers in heavy industries; the Chinese and Italians as *restaurateurs*; and so on. Although gross exaggerations, these stereotypes do point to the general trend for minorities to concentrate in unusually large numbers in certain special industrial sectors and, in the earlier stages of their settlement, for them to be found largely at the lower end of the occupational scale.

The reasons for these special trends may be mentioned here briefly. It was pointed out earlier on that in addition to the 'push factors' of unemployment, low living standards and the lack of opportunities in the countries of origin of immigrants, there were also the 'pull-factors' in Britain.[27] An expanding economy meant that this country could, except in periods of heavy unemployment, accommodate new entrants into its labour force. This applied to the nineteenth century when the Irish came in large numbers, the period 1890–1914 when the bulk of the Jews arrived, and the 1950s and 1960s when most of the coloured people came to Britain. Moreover, the post-war period of reconstruction and full employment induced the British authorities to actively recruit workers from the ranks of displaced East Europeans. When this source was exhausted other Europeans and especially Cypriots filled the gap. But the vacancies to be filled by the newcomers were in jobs which the English were reluctant to fill, the menial unskilled tasks, the lower paid skilled jobs, and some marginal trades and occupations.

It is now necessary to give a concise factual account of the employment situations of various minority groups. It may then be possible to draw certain comparisons and conclusions. Let us start with the more recent immigrants. In the first place we find that among the coloured male population aged fifteen years and over a larger proportion are economically active, that is in employment or seeking employment, than among the general population. The reasons seem to be that in the English population a bigger proportion receive higher education and enter employment at a later age, plus the fact that the English have an older age structure, as noted in Chapter 2, hence more of them have retired from work. The educational factor is, however, also prevalent among African men as against other coloured groups, especially in London. This is because of the large number of Africans who came to study in Britain. To illustrate this, in London 94.5 per cent of the Jamaican men were economically active but compared with only 64.9 per cent of West Africans in 1966. Comparative figures for other groups are: total population 85.8 per cent, Cypriots 89.4 per cent, Indians 88.5 per cent and Pakistanis 89.9 per cent. The situation for women is somewhat different. Jamaican and Caribbean women generally are still economically active in far larger numbers than are English women: well over 60 per cent as against 42 per cent in the general population. More West Indian women seem to have their children looked after by others and some still have their children in the West Indies. The percentages for Indians, Pakistanis and Cypriots are much nearer the general average.[28]

Taking now the longer established minority groups, we find that in the 1950s and 1960s Jewish men and women had economic activity rates lower than the general population. For men the proportion was not very much lower, 80 per cent as against 86 per cent respectively, and this could be accounted for by a much higher percentage of Jewish young people staying on in full-time education after the age of 15 years. For the women the difference was far greater: in one middle-class suburb of London, densely populated with Jews, only 22 per cent of the Jewish women were economically active against 40 per cent in the general female population of the district. This could be explained primarily by the traditional view amongst Jews that the married woman's place is in the home.[29] Both Polish and Irish men, in the early 1960s, were above the English as far as the proportions of the economically active were concerned: 87 per cent and 90 per cent respectively. As far as the women were concerned the Poles had a lower proportion – 36 per cent; and the Irish a higher one – 53 per cent.[30] Of course in all these cases the age-structure and marital status of the population will affect percentages. As we saw in Chapter 2 the Irish, although taken as an ethnic group the oldest established minority, have their ranks continually replenished with young unmarried people, which is not the case with either the Jews or the Poles. It is the youthfulness of the Irish population and the large numbers who are not married which give the high economic activity rates for both males and females.

The occupational and industrial distributions of the various minority groups show that the kind of stereotypes mentioned above are certainly false. Yet some industrial concentrations *are* discernible and the general trend for lower status occupations to be more widespread especially among recent immigrants is also borne out by the facts. Thus, in the total male population of Greater London only 6 per cent are unskilled labourers and in the West Midlands conurbation the figure is 7.8 per cent. As against this we get the high figures of 20.7 per cent labourers among Jamaicans in the London area and 22.9 per cent in the West Midlands, where this is surpassed by 26.6 per cent of labourers among Indians and the phenomenally high figure of 53 per cent among the Pakistanis. However, it is also true that at the other end of the scale we find fairly high proportions of professional people among some of the immigrant groups. Thus in the London area 18 per cent of Indians, 17.5 per cent of West Africans and 12.3 per cent of Pakistanis were in this category.[31] The profession highly represented by Asian immigrants is medicine. It has been reported that 18 per cent of doctors recruited to general practice in Britain in 1967–8 and the first half of 1969 had Asian qualifications, compared with 4 per cent in 1961–2. In Birmingham, for instance, there is the even higher recruitment figure of 27 per cent.[32] Similarly among women the immigrants are highly represented in some professional services such as nursing: 16.3 per cent of nurses in the West Midlands and 13.5 per cent in Greater London were West Indian in 1966. But as with men, the more recent immigrant women are found in much greater numbers in the unskilled or semi-skilled factory jobs than are English women, and this applies in particular to the Jamaican and Cypriot women.[33]

The industrial distribution shows that immigrant groups were often heavily over-represented in some areas of the economy. Thus, there are large concentrations of West Indians in London in transport and communications, huge proportions of Indians and Pakistanis in the metal industries of the West Midlands, large numbers of Cypriots in catering services, and the single highest concentration of any group is in the London clothing industry which employs 60 per cent of the Cypriot female labour force. To highlight the concentrations we can also look at areas where some of the minority groups are under-represented. To give just a couple of examples: the Jamaicans are under-represented in particular in agriculture, coal-mining, public administration, the distributive trades and the professions; and few Cypriots are to be found in transport and other service industries.[34] Furthermore what is most significant is that looking at trends between 1961 and 1966 the Race Relations Report found that 'there was no sign whatever that the industrial distribution of male immigrant groups moved towards that of the total population.'[35] And they continue by saying that among the men the indicators suggested even further concentration although among the women there was a very slight move towards the industrial distribution of the general population. These points suggest that we ought to consider below both the causes and the effects of the special employment pattern of immigrants.

But first let us complete the picture by looking at the employment patterns of the earlier immigrant groups to see if any changes have occurred since their settlement in Britain. Among the Irish, for instance, in the earlier part of the nineteenth century the largest number were the harvesters who constituted a seasonal migrant labour force, that is workers most of whom did not settle in England or Scotland, but were engaged year-in-year-out for the harvesting period on the larger farms. Another growing category later on in the century was the Irish labour force engaged in canal and railway construction. These were the original 'navvies', workers who undertook the heaviest work and were engaged by subcontractors. By the nature of the work this labour force was geographically highly mobile but, unlike the harvesters, they mostly settled here. Among the permanent Irish settlers during the last century other occupations with fairly high proportions were: mining, building, portering, spinning and weaving, and work in the docks and fruit markets. Among the women the largest number entered domestic service. The concentrations in the areas mentioned were quite intense and the influence on the pattern of employment among the Irish is to be felt right up to the present day. The continuity of the basic pattern described resulted from the needs of the British economy eliciting similar kinds of recruitment. For instance during the Second World War, despite travel restrictions between Britain and Eire which was neutral, there was great demand for Irish labour in agriculture and some sectors of industry. The reconstruction period since the war meant that Irish labour was again sought for rebuilding the bombed cities and the improvement of the communication lines. J. A. Jackson sums up the position thus:

The majority of the Irish entered those types of employment which were unacceptable to many British workers and . . . the new arrival from Ireland was more mobile in his search for employment than the native worker. Unskilled work with long hours characteristically absorbed the Irish immigrants. Heavy labour in the building industry, railway and road construction and maintenance, and in the heavy and more deleterious branches of metal and chemical manufacture, were the typical avenues of employment for men – jobs which often had little appeal to the British worker.[36]

Yet despite the persistence of the pattern it would not be true to say that no diversification in the occupations of the Irish has taken place at all. The new trend, albeit limited, was initiated by the general shortage of labour during the war. Transport and other service jobs were being entered in fairly large numbers and by 1951 the Irish had an important stake in some of the professions: 11.5 per cent of doctors and 11.4 per cent of nurses and midwives in England and Wales were Irish.[37]

Until the later part of the nineteenth century the broad occupational distribution of the Jews was a three-tier one: the outdoor traders and artisans relying on such occupations as peddling, hawking and glaziery and forming the poorer group; the shopkeepers forming the economic group in the middle; and the merchants and financiers concerned mainly with international trade forming a small wealthy group.

A complete change took place following the arrival of the East European immigrants in the 1880s. These were mainly semi-skilled or unskilled artisans accustomed to small work-shops. England had a factory system with a sufficiently large reservoir of unskilled English and Irish labour, and few important industrial areas were undeveloped. Under such conditions the East European immigrant in London and other large towns soon had to re-establish the small workshop and gain a livelihood in a few trades partly known to him, which soon acquired the tag of 'Jewish occupations'. The staple occupation was tailoring, carried out in the notorious sweat-shop. Other typical occupations were boot, shoe and slipper making, furniture manufacturing, and cigar making. The concentrations were marked: in 1880 about a quarter of the Jewish workers in the East End of London were engaged in tailoring; by 1901 in London as many as 40 per cent of the men and 50 per cent of the women were in tailoring; 12.5 per cent of men were in footwear manufacturing and 10 per cent in furniture manufacturing. Smaller numbers were in service trades and worked as barbers, bakers, printers, grocers and watchmakers.[38]

Since the second quarter of the twentieth century and ex-tending up to the 1960s there has been a great deal of Jewish occupational diversification. This trend shows large numbers abandoning the semi-skilled manual occupations; increasing proportions entering occupations with opportunities for self-employment such as shopkeeping, hairdressing and taxi-driving and a continuous rise in the numbers of those entering the professions and general white-collar jobs. Two final points are important to mention concerning the Jews. First, due to new developments of large-scale production and distribution, where the Jewish entrepreneur was in the forefront, there are some signs that the trend towards self-employment is being reversed. This kind of modern business rationalization is affecting the small Jewish businessman, and more Jews are, therefore, once again entering paid employment. Second, despite the occupational diversification, the Jewish clusters on the industrial scene remain. To give some examples, the small Jewish clothier may be replaced by a Jewish salesman in the clothing industry, and the grocer by a manager in a chain of supermarket stores. At a quick glance Jews in Britain are found in large concentrations in the clothing and textile trades, distributive trades and light industries, and to an increasing degree around professional services and administration in general. On the whole, Jewish interest in finance has been reduced and preoccupation with manufacturing substantially increased. It is also the case that there is an under-representation of Jews in agriculture and heavy industries.[39]

The Polish minority resembles in some respects the other groups. First, like the Irish, they were in strong demand by British agriculture during and immediately after the Second World War, although many abandoned this sector of the economy as soon as they were able to – at the peak period in 1947 some 10 per cent of the Polish labour force was in agriculture. The favoured avenues of employment for Poles have been building, brick-making, coal-mining, engineering and work in the textile industry and in catering. At the end of the 1940s nearly 80 per cent were manual workers[40] which compares with practically the same proportion among the Irish in London in the 1960s.[41] What is interesting, however, is the wide spectrum covered by the white-collar group. A 1948 list includes substantial numbers of university professors and lecturers, schoolteachers, journalists and writers, lawyers, actors, musicians, painters and sculptors, architects, engineers in all branches, doctors and dentists, qualified chemists, civil servants, clerks and so on.[42] Within the non-manual category the Poles seem, from the very inception of their community in Britain, to have resembled more than most groups, except for the Jews,[43] the occupational distribution of the English.

The smaller minorities also show peculiar occupational patterns and industrial concentrations. Some of the coloured groups in seaports such as Cardiff and Liverpool are mainly connected with the shipping industry; the Sikh Indians are predominantly travelling salesmen; and there is a phenomenal concentration of Chinese in the catering trade. There are supposed to be between 150 and 200 Chinese restaurants in London alone and perhaps a thousand in the whole of England.[44]

Finally, another peculiarity found in the work pattern of minority groups is that, as a rule, a quite substantial proportion of their members are employed in what could be termed the 'internal economies' of the respective communities. To illustrate this many examples can be given. In the Jewish community, one of the best organized minorities, there are numerous professions and establishments connected simply with the community itself. There are the religious and educational bodies with their personnel; the charitable and political organizations with their civil servants; the Jewish food-stores, bakeries, butchers'-shops, restaurants and hotels purveying kosher products; the Jewish Press and other publishing bodies, and the Jewish student hostels. The Poles too are similarly endowed with their own newspapers and library facilities, social clubs, food-stores selling Polish and East European products, and Roman Catholic parishes ministering especially to Poles. Again, the Irish have large numbers of their group engaged in meeting their religious needs through the Catholic churches and convent schools: in 1951 26 per cent of the Roman Catholic priests and 31.5 per cent of the nuns were Irish-born.[45] In the Camden Town area the London Irish have their own dancehall, employment agency and community centre providing various services.[46] Finally one need only stroll through some London streets to observe for instance the food-stores and greengrocers' shops catering for the West Indians, and the numerous cafés owned and frequented almost exclusively by Cypriots; or again, the stores catering for Asians in places such as Southall and the East End of London.

It is possible to discern four principal reasons for the special employment structures found in the minorities here considered: (1) the minority's original economic background; (2) the needs of the general economy; (3) prejudice and discrimination by the majority; (4) the internal needs of the minority, a factor already considered above.

Regarding the first factor, we saw in Chapter 1 that some of the immigrants, such as the West Indians, the Irish, the Cypriots, the Indians and the Pakistanis, have a largely rural background; or in some cases they emanate from newly established urban centres in their native lands. Having had an agricultural or semi-urbanized environment they have had little experience of industrial skills, and the lack of skill is also a result of the low educational and training standards in the countries of origin. Consequently the majority have automatically found themselves in Britain in the lower-paid unskilled occupations. However, discrimination and the needs of the general economy have at times induced the employment of skilled immigrants in unskilled occupations. As for other minority groups, the effects of past backgrounds have similarly left their mark. The East European Jews in their countries of origin, such as Tsarist Russia or Poland, were not allowed either to own land or to live in the larger towns. This meant that the majority came from the *shtetl*, the small towns where livelihood was eked out from domestic industry and trading. Hence the small Jewish apparel-producing workshops in Britain of a few decades ago, in which the bulk of Jewish workers were employed, and the large number of merchants in this minority group at the time. Similarly some of the Asian immigrants, say the Sikhs and the Chinese, because of lack of substantial capital or special skills, have established themselves in small enterprises like restaurants, or as travelling salesmen.

Concerning the needs of the general economy we find that often through deliberate government policy foreign labour was recruited for those industries and those jobs in which they were most needed. This usually meant the lower paid ranks in the undermanned industries deserted by the better-off English worker, a trend particularly at the time of the early post-war reconstruction period when East European immigrants were directed into certain areas of the economy. But it is true that even in 'the absence of controls and direction, foreign labour tends to be absorbed by certain industries, in particular those which offer the most unpleasant jobs'.[47] It was recognized, however, early on after the war that: 'A shortage of persons qualified to fill professional and administrative posts may seriously impede the nation's recovery and its economic and social progress [and that therefore] highly qualified foreigners who can be persuaded to take up employment in this country will materially assist the recovery of industry, the expansion of exports, the administration of the new social services and the progress of research work in the natural and social sciences.'[48] The more recent Common-wealth Immigrants Acts have in fact accepted these principles and under B vouchers mainly doctors, dentists, science and technology graduates, teachers and nurses have been allowed in.[49] Yet even in these professions it is at the lower echelons that the new arrivals have been accommodated. This could be caused by both the actual level of skill being lower among the new immigrants, and a tendency to discriminate against them so as to reserve the better jobs for members of the majority population.

We now may consider the third factor, that is discrimination and prejudice in employment generally. There is a great deal of incontrovertible evidence that these factors function fairly potently in this field. The 1967 PEP Report showed that of 150 local employers interviewed 37 did not employ coloured people, and of these only 4 said that this was not for deliberate policy reasons. A breakdown of the total number not em-ploying coloured people shows that only 3 employers on the manufacturing side were involved, whilst in retail outlet the number was 22, and in service companies 12. Discrimination may be discerned in other ways. For instance nearly three-quarters of the coloured immigrants who were in government service in their countries of origin were employed in Britain in manufacturing industries in the capacity of unskilled and semi-skilled workers.[50] In other words background, mentioned above, is not the sole reason for the concentrations found in manual occupations; a good deal of downgrading also takes place. It was also suggested above that in the professions it is the lower paid jobs that the immigrants have to take and that this may be due partly to discrimination. Thus whilst about half the junior doctors working in hospitals were of immigrant birth, only about one-sixth of the senior registrars were. Again we remarked earlier on the very large numbers of coloured nurses, but in teaching hospitals they make up only one to two per cent of the total nursing staff.[51] On the whole the better jobs, those that bring the person face to face with the public as for instance in shops, banks and offices, and where responsibility is involved, are not being offered to the more recent immigrants.

It is claimed by the employers concerned that this is not purely colour prejudice, but rather out of the necessity of employing in such posts people fully conversant with the habits and temperaments of the majority. Thus the less anglicized Europeans, such as the Cypriots, are similarly very rarely employed in such capacities. What many regard as disturbing, however, is the fact that the second generation of the coloured minorities, the young people who were born in this country, who had their schooling here and have become anglicized, are still discriminated against particularly in so far as white-collar employment is concerned.[52] This is one reason why the Community Relations Commission set up in 1969 The Advisory Committee on Employment whose task it is to encourage equality of opportunity in all aspects of employment.[53]

The equality of opportunity depends primarily on the two sides of the labour market: the employer and organized labour. It is true that the Government can influence matters not only by indirect means such as the Community Relations Commission, but also more directly. The 1968 Race Relations Act does in fact do just that. Although the Act leaves certain employment situations outside its jurisdiction through its 'racial balance clause' which allows discrimination where it is 'for the purpose of securing or preserving a reasonable balance of persons of different racial groups employed in the undertaking', the other provisions of the Act do channel complaints to conciliation machinery and provide also for the possibility of civil proceedings for various types of discrimination in employment. It appears realistic for the Act to make employers liable for the unlawful actions of their employees unless they can prove that they have taken reasonable steps to prevent the employee from discriminating.[54]

But it is still doubtful whether the prejudices coming from the direction of organized labour can be sufficiently counteracted. While the Trades Union Congress time and again have reaffirmed their opposition to racial discrimination and at the national level trade unions adhere to this view, some leading trade unionists have been less sympathetic. Thus Lord Carron addressing his union was reported as claiming that the immigrants were taking out from the national wealth much more than their fair share by using the Welfare State to which they have not fully contributed.[55]

The weighing up of the material costs and benefits due to the recent influx of immigrants is a very complex exercise which is outside the purview of this book. It may be mentioned, however, that economists are by no means unanimous in their estimates and that such figures as have been calculated are as yet tentative in view of the dearth of factual information. Whilst some have argued that a large-scale inflow of immigrants leads to an increase in excess demand and is, therefore, inflationary and that it worsens the balance-of-payments position[56], others have stressed the overall beneficial effects as a result of immigrants boosting productivity.[57] Of course a distinction must be made between the economic impact of immigrants in the short-run and the long-run. The benefits do seem to accrue mainly in the short-run due to a number of factors: such as the proportionately large number of able-bodied immigrant workers, the comparatively low capital investment effected in their settlement here, and the proportionately lower immediate demand they make on the social services (see Table 4.2), a situation quite contrary to what Lord Carron believed it to be.

But despite some arguments showing certain positive contributions and beneficial effects of immigrants on the country's economy, at least in the short run, it is the more pessimistic views, stressing the strain on the country, which seem to hold sway over public opinion. And in trade union circles the kind of view expressed by Carron still abounds particularly at the local level. The rank and file still regard the coloured worker as a competitor, at best as a kind of 'reserve', the first to go in case of unemployment, one who has to take second best, and one who is not to be treated equally when promotion is in question. Membership of trade unions does not help. In fact a higher proportion of members had experienced discrimination than of the non-members. The PEP Report gave 42 per cent for coloured union members who had been refused jobs purely because of race or colour, and only 34 per cent with similar experiences among the non-members.[58]

TABLE 4.2: *Immigrants and the Social Services**
Cost per head of Social Services, 1961–1981†

	Health and welfare	Education and child care	National insurance and assistance benefits	Tota
1961		£ at 1961 prices		
Total population	18·5	12·4	31·2	62·1
Immigrant population	18·4	13·3	19·2	50·9
1966				
Total population	18·6	12·1	31·7	62·4
Immigrant population	17·4	13·9	17·4	48·7
1981				
Total population ..	19·0	15·3	33·5	67·8
A. (*b*)Immigrant .. population ..	16·9	21·6	19·1	57·6
B. (*c*)Immigrant population ..	16·8	22·9	18·1	57·9

* Reproduced from the *National Institute Economic Review*.[59]
† Current expenditure and grants; assuming no further net immigration; assuming some continued immigration.

To sum up the situation with regard to employment among the coloured minorities, one must agree with the conclusions of the Race Relations Report. They say:

The one fact that stands out above all others is that throughout the field of employment, discrimination is widespread and pervasive. It manifests itself in recruitment, training, promotion, and a host of other ways. This discrimination is not the result of any centrally inspired policy of government, unions or employers' organizations, but is determined by decisions at the local level.[60]

Considering the paramount importance of the local situation it is not surprising to find peculiar 'bunchings' in the employment patterns of coloured immigrants. Thus many Midlands companies have used special 'go-betweens' to recruit new workers from particular ethnic groups. Once entrenched sufficiently these groups come to control fresh recruitment and promotion.[61] Similarly public employers have sometimes used special arrangements for recruiting from certain groups, a good example being London Transport and its recruitment of West Indians. The upshot of our consideration of the discrimination factor is that this leads, as we see in the case of the more recent immigrants, to certain concentrations determined often by local conditions and to a relegation into inferior types of jobs.

The situation has been somewhat similar in the case of European minority groups in the earlier stages of their settlement. Jerzy Zubrzycki mentioned the unfavourable attitude expressed by English workers towards the Poles.[62] Due to this factor even today concentrations are clearly discernible in some industrial areas and in some firms. In Croydon, an area studied by Sheila Patterson, nearly half of the Polish men worked in one firm, some sections of which were virtually Polish preserves.[63] This was the case some twenty years after large-scale Polish settlement in Britain, and in some respects was similar to another firm employing over fifty per cent of West Indians working in the heavy industrial sector.[64] Again in the case of Jews much has been written about the disabilities experienced by them during the last century and the great extent to which discrimination in the economic field was exerted against them earlier in this century. But even more recently discrimination has been found in some sections of the economy. The reports of the Trades Advisory Council based on records gathered between 1945 and 1955 deal with four main types of economic discrimination: (a) discrimination in employment: the Council investigated 163 separate instances of refusals by employers to employ Jews; (b) discrimination in trade: boycotting of Jewish firms by non-Jewish firms was found to be rare; (c) discrimination in services: in this category a practice which has lingered on was that of denying Jewish customers insurance or credit facilities; (d) discrimination by Trade Association or Trade Union – no Trade Unions were found to refuse to admit Jewish members, whilst local Trade Associations rather than national bodies were sometimes the discriminators against Jewish traders.[65] To focus on just one analogy again, the discrimination in insurance and credit facilities is somewhat similar to the kind experienced by coloured minorities mentioned in the 1967 PEP Report.[66]

The special occupational structure which has developed amongst these minorities has two major effects and a number of secondary repercussions. First, there is the factor of partial segregation; second, the higher rate of unemployment. These features emerge in contemporary society mainly among the more recently settled groups, but they were also seen in the earlier phases of settlement of older minorities. Segregation appears both in terms of industry, so that some industries become associated with immigrant or minority groups and in terms of firms in that some employers, both public and private, are known to employ immigrants whilst others are notorious among minority group members for their reluctance to do so. Segregation within the firm is further evidenced by the existence of ethnic work-units and the separation of facilities. Bob Hepple discusses some of the secondary effects of such segregation leading to all sorts of conflicts and difficult industrial relations.[67] But it must be stressed that for many minority members the segregation is imposed in a number of ways: in terms of ethnic work-units in the general economy: in terms of employment in firms owned by members of the same ethnic group but serving the general public; or in terms of employment in the 'internal economy' of the group. These segregated avenues of employment may be trodden because of language and other cultural difficulties or simply because it is easier to get work in this way. However, the attitudes of local Trade Unions and English workers in general have not always been helpful in ameliorating the situation.

The second major effect, as we have said, is unemployment. Despite the mainly favourable official pronouncements made by Trade Unions and employers' associations; despite the clearer approach by the Ministry of Labour and employment exchanges in holding over the employers known to discriminate the ultimate sanction of withdrawing exchange facilities; and despite the measures in the Race Relations Act, the incidence of unemployment is consistently higher among new immigrants than among the English. This is because the principle at the shop-floor level of 'last in, first out' is still observed, so that redundancy in times of economic depression is bound to be felt particularly among the newly established groups. Some of these groups, having also extraordinarily high proportions of unskilled workers, are bound to be affected more harshly by automation. And there are also informal 'quotas', varying between three per cent and ten per cent, agreed upon by management and unions.[68] The situation among men in London as analysed by R. B. Davison from the 1961 Census figures is given in Table 4.3.

The 1961 data show that in the case of women unemployment was still relatively high among West Indians and Poles but not quite so high among the Irish and the Cypriots. Another way of comparing unemployment is to see what percentage of the total unemployed is accounted for by

TABLE 4.3: *Unemployment by ethnic group – London, April 1961*[69]

Ethnic Group:	Males – %
English	3·2
Jamaican	7·4
Other Caribbean	6·0
Indian	4·4
Pakistani	5·4
Polish	4·2
Irish	4·8
Cypriot	5·8

minority workers. Such a calculation is given for the period 1963–8 in connexion with coloured groups and this shows that 'in times of rising unemployment Commonwealth immigrants tend to be harder hit than the general population'.[70] The very unfavourable position of West Indians as far as unemployment is concerned is matched for this group also by their least favourable socio-economic status not only *vis-à-vis* the English population,[71] but also as compared with other minorities, including coloured ones. The 1966 Census showed that the West Indians had the lowest proportions as employers, managers, professionals and other non-manual workers. Conversely they had the highest proportion as manual workers and what is most significant is that within the latter category, together with the Pakistanis, they had the highest proportion in unskilled positions and the fewest foremen and supervisors. Now, this does not tally with the assessment of skill possessed by West Indians given by British managers (see Table 4.4 below). Regarding this the West Indians appear in a superior position as compared with other groups, yet they get relatively fewer of the skilled jobs and supervisory tasks than, say, the Indians.

TABLE 4.4: *Managerial Assessment of the Skill Level of coloured workers*[72]

Nationality	More skilled than British workers	About the same as British workers – %	Less skilled than British workers – %	No. of firms responding
West Indians	o	44	56	39
Pakistanis	o	21	79	19
Indians	o	37	63	33
Arabs	o	23	77	13
Africans	o	27	73	11

Given the low socio-economic position of West Indians and the inconsistency of this fact with the level of skill they are supposed to possess, Peter Collison suggests that 'one might be tempted to argue that British society discriminates more sharply against people of darker skins and evidence from other societies might be adduced to support this view'.[73] Peter Wright suggests another explanation: this is that precisely because they are more skilled, have no language difficulties and expect a fuller acceptance by the British, the latter reject this demand and counteract by expecting them to fulfil lower status roles.[74]

The essential question is to what extent the less favourable urban conditions, that is poor housing, inferior jobs and higher rates of unemployment, also apply to the descendants of immigrants – the West Indians and the other coloured groups. There is insufficient information to elucidate this point for most of the minority groups, but some indications of trends and a limited comparison is possible by considering certain aspects of social mobility.

Social Mobility

From the above account one could reach the hypothetical conclusion that some minority groups appear to be caught in a vicious circle from which they cannot escape. Their social advancement seems to be barred because of the situation in which they find themselves. To put it bluntly, the problem is this. Bad housing, more unemployment, work in lower paid manual jobs and large families add up to an unfavourable environment for the educational needs of the children of these minority groups. And the home environmental problem is hardly counteracted by the school. Geographical concentration of these groups in slum areas means that immigrant children will be over-represented in some schools, and that the problems of adapting children from rural or other very different backgrounds to life in the urban-industrial centres of Britain will be accentuated. Furthermore there are language difficulties in many cases. To make things worse, fewer facilities and teachers are available in such areas, problems already faced by working-class children generally. The assertion is then made on behalf of the indigenous population that 'The chief cause of racial tension is not housing, personal habits, or fear of "cheap labour" but the nagging fear that children will be held back at school by immigrant children whose standards of literacy and intelligence are much lower'.[75] This kind of prejudice completes the picture of an impasse, as a result of which inter-generational mobility seems well nigh impossible for minorities.

The ingredients of the kind of situation described above were present in the case of earlier minorities and non-coloured groups as much as they are today in the case of the more recent coloured immigrants. Thus, in the Leeds 'ghetto' at the turn of the century four of the board schools were attended almost exclusively by Jewish children who formed the vast majority of the 1,400 Jewish children receiving general education in the city.[76] Alternatively segregation and concentration were produced by Jewish-run schools such as the Jews' Free School in the East End of London.[77] The educational opportunities for Jews were probably worse, and certainly were no better, than in the mid-1960s, say, for the Indian children in a primary school in Southall where they constituted 60 per cent of the school population,[78] or the 10 schools in Islington each of which had over 40 per cent immigrant children, making up a total of 6,000, half of which were Greek or Turkish speaking Cypriots.[79] The speaking of a foreign language applied to Poles in Bradford in the 1950s or to Jews in Manchester early on in this century as much as to the more recently settled minorities, whilst the disadvantages of having a working-class background were probably experienced more intensely by the Irish than by most of the coloured groups. Yet, as we shall see below, the Irish, the Poles and the Jews have achieved high rates of social mobility, having appreciably improved their socio-economic conditions and social status within a few decades. For instance 17.8 per cent of the Irish in a 1966 London sample were found to be in the 'middle class', defined in terms of non-manual occupations, whilst only 5.3 per cent of West Indians could be so classed in a comparable sample.[80] Using the same criteria and comparable samples for the early 1960s in a study of the London suburb of Edgware, it was found that the Jews there had 64 per cent in the 'middle class' and thus surpassed the general population of the district of which only 59 per cent were found to be so classed.[81]

Now, it is true that a survey in two working-class districts of London, Stepney and Hackney, showed that in the 1960s there were still substantial numbers of Jews in lower socio-economic positions: Jews who felt they could not aspire to very much higher standards and could not reach the more affluent districts of London.[82] Yet the changes in the geographical distribution of Jews, both in London and the provinces, shows clearly that for very large numbers it has been possible to move to more affluent districts. As evidenced in several studies, the ecological aspect of the upward mobility for Jews suggests that the movement has been extremely rapid. In addition there are other relevant data concerning the attainment of middle-class rank found in a readership survey of the *Jewish Chronicle*, relating to the late 1950s, and a study of leisure among Jewish teenagers in the 1960s. The findings reveal the very high standards attained in the levels of consumption and travelling and particularly the high level of household amenities.[83] Most of the changes in the socio-economic structure of the Jews have been in line with general trends in the larger society, the difference being that these changes have been more accentuated and have taken place more rapidly among Jews.

Another minority which has succeeded in moving up the social scale quite rapidly has been the Polish group. In a study carried out on the outskirts of South London by Sheila Patterson, a mere fifteen years after the bulk of the Poles settled in Britain, this investigator found that:

The Poles who came to Croydon to live were already fairly well-established in civilian life and this move often represented a step up from the poorer housing in Brixton, Peckham and Battersea which was all the majority had been able to afford in the first years of settlement. It also illustrated the upward mobility that is characteristic of this particular exile group and its members' tendency to follow the southward or south-westward movement of upwardly mobile Londoners.[84]

The majority of the Poles in Croydon had in fact reached middle-class positions and similar situations can be found in most of the British towns where Polish groups have settled.

The Irish, too, have proved their ability to move from the extremes of poverty in the middle of the nineteenth century to improved living standards by the beginning of this century. Their social advancement was intertwined with their contributions to the labour movement as successful trade union leaders and left-wing politicians in British life. There is, however, also a fairly strong middle-class Conservative element in the Irish community reflected by the thousands of members of smart Irish clubs which exist in most of the large cities and cater exclusively for the social needs of the Irish professional man, the well-to-do businessman or those with other white-collar occupations.[85]

In contrast we find the more recently settled immigrant groups, in particular the coloured ones, to have made only modest advances in some respects, as exemplified by the slightly improved levels of housing amenity of West Indians.

Or they have made no progress whatever in their employment situations, as comparative data for 1961 and 1966 suggest.[86] It is necessary, therefore, to explain why differences in social mobility obtain not only between the newer minorities and the older ones but also, say, between the Jewish minority and the indigenous population itself, that is the English majority. One suggestion could be the time factor. It could be argued that the coloured minorities have not been here long enough to have had a chance to improve themselves appreciably. Another factor of importance may be the state of the economy at the time of settlement, which would explain how the Poles advanced their socio-economic status rapidly in a period of post-war reconstruction and the relative prosperity of the 1950s, whilst the coloured immigrants were occupationally almost immobile during the economically depressed conditions in the first half of the sixties. But neither of these factors is sufficient to explain the highly improved position of the Jewish minority relative to the indigenous majority. Some, like Lord Snow, would argue that the success of the Jews is due to the extraordinarily favourable genetic inheritance of that minority.[87] The lack of such inherited abilities in some groups, say, the coloured minorities, could by the same token be invoked as an explanation for their non-favourable socio-economic conditions.

Now, what is the scientific truth in this matter? Geneticists and psychologists have undertaken a great deal of work in this field, yet their conclusions are far from clear. There is general agreement that the races of mankind are not pure,[88] but the category 'race' does designate a group of people characterized by certain concentrations in regard to frequency and distribution of hereditary genes or physical character.[89] However, a physical classification thus derived provides 'no basis for believing that the groups of mankind differ in their innate capacity for intellectual and emotional development'.[90] Michael Banton who reviewed the work of geneticists concludes that in the processes of natural selection there is an interplay between race and culture, but that it is culture rather than race which explains mental characteristics.[91]

This contention does not necessarily deny the intrinsic

hereditary nature of, say, intelligence, but it does deny that race as such determines the *distribution* of intelligence. It is even less clear what actually is meant by 'intelligence' and how one can achieve strict comparability between a variety of cultures or sub-cultures, in measuring intelligence which must be regarded as 'a fluid collection of overlapping abilities, rather than any single identifiable faculty'.[92] And whilst some psychological experiments, such as rearing identical twins in different environments or studying the IQs of children in orphanages, seem to point to the importance of heredity,[93] other experiments show how culturally conditioned expectations influence actual performance. In the celebrated experiment by Rosenthal and Jacobson schoolchildren were subjected to certain tests by these psychologists. Their teachers were not told that these were dummy tests but were informed in confidence that certain children, who were in fact randomly selected, would show marked gains in their intelligence in the coming year. When these children were retested with genuine tests it was found that they *did* gain more than the rest.[94] Similar situations are said to apply in multi-racial situations. Where some races are regarded as of inferior intelligence, they will in fact put up an inferior performance. The socio-cultural climate influences their performance which then fits the expectations, despite the distinct possibility that potentially their intelligence is the same as that of the rest.

To deny the influence of racial characteristics as a determining factor, so far as mental characteristics are concerned, is not to deny that certain selective processes, along other than racial lines, do take place. Thus a certain concentration of people with high mental ability will be found in some strata of society as a result of the selective processes of social mobility. In the case of some minority groups such as the Jews, who are not a distinct racial group,[95] both selective processes and cultural factors will leave their mark. Thus, their high degree of achievement can be explained as follows. First, there is the immediate cultural environment mentioned by Paul Vincent who studied the measured intelligence of Glasgow Jewish schoolchildren, whose scores were much higher than those of non-Jewish children in the city. He suggests that favourable aspects of this environment are the wider stimulating experience of Jewish children in their homes and youth organizations and the fact that they share in two cultures, the Hebrew and the West European.[96] The question is, though, how did Jewish homes or Jewish parents come to provide the greater stimulus for their children? Here we must invoke the historical fact of the enormous selective pressures to which Jews have been subjected over very long periods of time. Even over a shorter period Vincent shows how Glasgow Jews and their antecedents have been subjected to selective processes through migrations from Eastern Europe and within Britain, resulting in a group of people with high initiative and ability.[97] The pertinent point here is that Jews have become more thoroughly urbanized. In many parts of Europe they were not allowed to own land, and even in industry and trade they were pushed into peripheral or new enterprises. For these reasons they could thrive best in growing urban areas and they became highly conditioned to the faster tempo and fluid nature of industrial society.[98]

It would appear, therefore, that in the case of the newer, coloured minorities whose backgrounds have been much less urban-industrial,[99] time would tell. The coming generations would be much more attuned to their surroundings and be able to improve their socio-economic standing sufficiently to bring them on a par with the rest of the population. Presumably it is in order to hasten this process that particular efforts have been made in providing compensatory education to immigrants. In a contribution in this field by the Community Relations Commission's Advisory Committee on Education it is in fact stated clearly that one of their principal aims is 'to enable educationists to help immigrant children and adults develop basic technical and social skills'[100] to a higher degree so that they can adapt better to their new environment. Evidence from the United States suggests, however, that even if environment *was* all-important it would be over-optimistic to expect dramatic results from such compensatory education programmes. As Bryan Silcock puts it, the adverse environmental influences could not easily be corrected by such programmes.[101] Finally, there is prejudice and discrimination on account of colour which prevents social mobility among the newer minorities. It is true that this kind of obstacle was met by other minorities too – moreover regarding Jews it has been said that they achieved a high degree of social mobility precisely *because* they strove so hard to overcome their minority status. The contention is, however, that discrimination against coloured minorities is of a different order from discrimination against other minorities. The evidence given in terms of the larger numbers of coloured people discriminated against as compared with members of other minorities in similar situations[102] seems to underprop such an argument. And once again it is difficult to say what will be the effect of the educational and other public relations efforts directed at the majority and aimed at reducing colour prejudices. On the whole no confident assertions can be made regarding the extent to which the newer minorities will be able to catch up in socio-economic terms with the older European minorities and the rest of the population in this country. But as Michael Banton warns: 'If the second generation of immigrant children are not enabled to compete fairly with their age-mates for work and housing they may prove a rebellious and expensive minority'.[103] A situation such as this could prove detrimental to the development of the urban centres in an industrialized country like Britain. It is, therefore, essential to analyse the dynamic processes at work in these industrial cities.

Urban development and change

We have considered in this chapter the socio-economic conditions of various minorities from the early part of the nineteenth century right up to the late 1960s. This period covers the continually accelerated growth and increasing complexity of industrial-urban life as well as the multiplication of ethnic minority groups in the urban centres. The same period has also witnessed the rise in importance of these minorities not only from the point of view of their size but much more so as contributors to the development and change of urban life. We may be reminded here by the writings of Robert Park that cities have always been cosmopolitan meeting places of different races and cultures useful to one another and bringing about the extension and diffusion of urban culture and civilization.[104] But although Park recognized the changing nature of our industrial civilization he analysed its urban facet in terms of a social equilibrium. This may become disturbed but after a transitional period the balance is restored. He saw the city as having a symbiotic nature – being a super-organism into which various cultures and minority groups fit.

More recently there has been a shift from such integrationist theories to conflict theories. These, too, view urban life as complex systems but the accent is on the pressures exerted by the various interest groups within the system. The conflicting interests are seen most clearly in the context of ethnic relations, particularly in the underprivileged 'zone of transition'. As John Rex says this is 'a world far from the functionally integrated social systems . . . Only as sociologists begin to understand it will they begin to understand what the city is like on its underside'.[105] What actually happens to the ethnic sub-communities in the city and how they inter-relate with the wider society will be discussed in the final chapter.

The employment and housing situations of the various minorities described above showed a good deal of similarity for all the groups so far as the earlier phases of their settlement is concerned. This is so whether we consider the sub-standard housing, the segregated zones or ghettos, employment at the lower end of the scale, the peculiar industrial distribution, problems of education and so on. It is also the case that most of the minorities can be seen as having played important roles in the life and development of Britain's urban areas. The role was important even if it meant acting as replacement labour and being used frequently in marginal occupations. Whilst social mobility was experienced by a number of the longer established groups these still retain their minority status and encounter a certain amount of discrimination in the housing and labour markets, and in trading and service facilities.

The more recently formed coloured groups similarly bear a minority status and they suffer the added disadvantage of experiencing little or no social mobility out of the socio-economic positions they occupy, which are the lowest in British society. The ex-colonial worker does not seem able to rise a great deal socially in metropolitan society. An analysis of the social structure of this society in its urban-industrial setting suggests that it contains a major inconsistency. Its system makes contradictory demands: it motivates people to aspire to a higher status by achieving membership of higher socio-economic categories; yet it does not allow all to gain higher status, for it provides unequal opportunities for social mobility.[106]

The unequal opportunities apply not only to the newer coloured groups but also to other minorities and to large segments of the majority itself. However, large numbers of these other groups were enabled to escape from the lower strata. It is difficult to establish whether this was simply due to the appearance of new waves of immigrants which, by filling in the lower positions, enabled the older established groups to make their way up the social scale. The processes involved are probably more complex than this. One indication that older minorities are not simply pushed up from below by newer ones is that in the United States the Puerto Ricans who arrived *after* the Negroes have been socially more mobile than the Negroes. It has been suggested that the Puerto Ricans have more unified families and better ethnic organizations, hence their greater ability to break the cycle of discrimination.[107] It has also been suggested, however, that it is those Puerto Ricans who can be classed as 'whites' who experience less discrimination.[108] On the whole, the fact remains that in this country, as in America, the coloured groups are still relegated to the slum areas and the least desirable menial tasks. The division of society along a 'colour line' super-imposed on the general stratification system is shown diagrammatically below.[109]

Fig. 3A shows the 'caste line' which has operated over a long period in the southern states of the USA[110]. In the present British situation however, shown in Fig. 3B, the dividing line becomes tilted upwards. This 'colour line' does not set the non-white population rigidly below the top stratum, but it

FIGURE 3A: *The Caste Line**

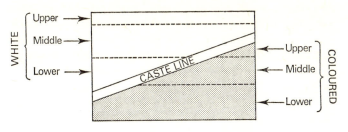

FIGURE 3B: *The Colour Line*

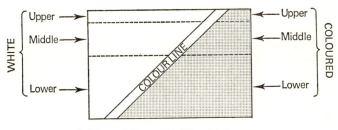

* Adapted from W. Lloyd Warner.

still depresses the vast majority of coloured people, giving their social class composition a skewed effect, which is due to discrimination as well as to less resourcefulness and lack of training among them. In other words, Britain has certainly no 'caste line' in that some coloured people are in the top reaches of its social scale, but it does have a 'colour line' which prevents a quick adjustment to a 'normal' social class distribution among the newer immigrants.

John Rex has argued that the coloured proletariat together with other underprivileged groups in the 'zone of transition', such as the newer Irish immigrants and smaller depressed sections of the indigenous population, form what effectively is a new housing class. But despite their similar socio-economic conditions alliances across class lines take place,[111] with race and ethnicity becoming intervening variables. The coloured groups may therefore become further isolated even within these sectors of the city. We shall see in our concluding analysis (Chapter 5) how they react to this situation and how they seek immediate security by reliance on their kinship structure, on communal organization and on religious ties. In addition their condition is ameliorated by agencies working on behalf of the wider society. Recent examples of this are the regional conferences organized by the Community Relations Commission 'to discuss the Government's urban aid programme for helping the socially deprived sections of the population'[112] and in immediately practical terms the increased aid given for instance to the city of Birmingham to enable it to appoint more Community Relations Officers.[113]

Such steps do not merely scratch the surface, as some sceptics believe. As Gunnar Myrdal argues, these factors, because of the *cumulative effects* they set in motion, will determine the direction in which minority-majority relations will go and in effect will shape the future of our urban centres.[114] To take Myrdal's example: if the standard of living of a coloured group is allowed to be lowered this will increase the prejudices of the whites which will further depress the group and so on; on the other hand a rise in employment will raise the group's standards, which may in the long run result in less discrimination meted out by the majority and less acrimony felt by the minority. Over any period of time the factors at work are numerous and the various influences may, as Myrdal says, 'turn the system around on its axis'.[115] If this were to happen Rex's assessment might be true. He says: 'The situation in the zone of transition is a highly unstable one and in any sudden crisis ethnic and class conflicts which are temporarily contained may crystallize and be pursued by more violent means'.[116] In other words the chance that the system might be pushed towards open conflict cannot by any means be excluded. Is there a possibility, though, that the 'zone of transition' will be dissolved in a new type of urban community – the plural society?

5 What is the Future?

In the foregoing chapters the reader will have been struck
by similarities found regarding many facets of the situations of
the ethnic minorities considered. There are, undoubtedly,
differences too, but the similarities are numerous and sufficiently deep to warrant a comparative approach[1] in an attempt now
to draw the strands together. This exercise will in the first
instance be retrospective, but my aim is to analyse the material
in the light of a general theoretical framework which is slowly
emerging in the sociology of inter-ethnic group relations. Such
an approach should enable us to get some idea of the prospects:
by highlighting the trends in minority-majority relations
we may gain an inkling of the future of certain ethnic sub-
communities in the context of British society.

Although some operational definitions were given early on,[2]
and conclusions were reached on such ubiquitous aspects
of ethnic relations as prejudice,[3] we must now redefine our
position. Thus, to say that an ethnic minority is a distinguishable group within a larger society on account of physical,
cultural or other characteristics, and that it is singled out for
discriminatory treatment by the dominant group in society is
correct descriptively; but to understand the essence of ethnic
minorities one must tackle the *dynamic situations* which dominant-subordinate group relations entail. As we have done in
Chapter 3 we must ask, for instance, why prejudices develop
in such contexts. The answer was given in terms of two inter-
acting factors: culture contact between the newly settled
ethnic groups and the indigenous population heightens ethnocentrism and simultaneously legitimizes the efforts of dominant groups to exploit the weaker minorities. The 'need' to
exploit or blame the ethnic minorities appears particularly at

times of economic crisis or periods of radical change in the industrial and social life of a society. This is well illustrated by historical facts. The rise of hostile attitudes towards minorities has occurred at such troubled times, instanced by the bitterness shown towards the Irish in the 1830s and 1840s, the anti-Semitic insults endured by Jews at the turn of the century and in the 1930s, and the anti-colour prejudices prevalent in the 1960s (see above Chapter 3, pp. 55f.). The American sociologist R. A. Schermerhorn is, therefore, right in asserting that 'prejudice [is] a product of *situations*, historical situations, economic situations, political situations; it is not a little demon that emerges in people simply because they are depraved'.[4]

This is not in any way to deny the repercussions of heightened prejudice on society as a whole and particularly on its minority groups singled out for such treatment. It does mean, however, that prejudice, discrimination and hostility must be viewed as dependent variables. Just the same the effects of hostile attitudes towards ethnic minorities will be real enough. One such effect is to weld them into greater cohesiveness. We have seen how discrimination in housing will lead to the creation of segregated zones for various minorities. These are not 'happy little communities' as Burgess and Park described them,[5] but rather 'zones of stagnation, festering slums' in which people are forced to stay.[6] The imposed segregation does, however, engender a community feeling, which even when social mobility takes place is often perpetuated by the minority moving *en bloc* to better districts. The sheer number living in close proximity stimulates minority organization, greater reliance on the kinship patterns, religious and cultural values, an internal economy, and generally a turning inwards which helps to perpetuate the group. Discrimination in employment, in education and recreation and in politics, and above all the bar put up against intermarriage have similar effects to residential segregation. These external factors reinforce each other and produce instances of extreme ethnocentric feelings developing within the minority group, leading, as we have seen above,[7] even to militancy.

It is wrong to imagine, however, that the cohesiveness

of ethnic minorities and their overall objectives are determined solely by the xenophobic attitudes and actions of the dominant group. There are internal forces at work which will contribute equally, if not more, to the processes of identification of minority members with their own groups. The strong kinship ties and sociability patterns amongst Jews, the Irish, the Africans, Indians and Pakistanis; the force of Judaism, albeit somewhat reduced, among Jews, of Pentecostal sects among West Indians, of Catholicism among the Poles and the Irish; and the ramifications of organizational life among Jews and Poles in particular, but not inconsiderable among the Irish and the newer coloured groups – these are all certain facets of communal life which reflect the general ethos of the minority.

One can think in terms of internal channels or means of identification available to group members, namely kinship, religion, organization (recreational, political, cultural, etc.). The use made of these is strongly influenced by the ethos of the group and its general feeling of peoplehood. In this respect the minorities we have considered differ substantially. Thus, the Poles are primarily a political group – they wish to return to Poland in order to recreate the political system of pre-war days.[8] If the political goals of such a group seem to become unattainable, or have to be put off for a long time, a radical weakening process overtakes the minority. Zubrzycki in fact maintains that for such reasons the Polish minority, if given occasion by being fully accepted in English society, is likely to disintegrate in the long run. In contrast, the underlying reason for the existence of the Irish and coloured minorities is economic – often simply the quest for work. In the case of the Irish, proximity to Ireland has produced an ethos based on a strong sentiment of loyalty to the original home.[9] As for the coloured immigrants their 'visibility' has helped to draw them together into self-conscious social groups.[10] There are distinctive cultural factors also at work, not only proximity to the original home for the Irish or 'colour' as far as, say, West Indians are concerned, but without these main factors, not accounting at the moment for external constraints, identification with their groups is likely to wane quite rapidly.

The Jews differ from the minorities so far mentioned, in that the reason for their existence is much more complex. Religious persecution, political inequality and lack of economic opportunities have all contributed to driving Jews to Britain from their previous places of residence. Furthermore, their previous status was similarly that of a minority, a factor that does not apply, say, to the Poles, although ex-colonial status which does apply to most coloured groups is comparable. It is also true that when the immigrant generations arrived, whatever group they belonged to, they had the common factor of being 'foreigners'. But Jews were already accustomed to this status as a result of their long history of migration from country to country. Their basic religious 'difference' in Christian Europe and the long tradition of minority status produced what appear to be more powerful factors of identification than the factors produced by the backgrounds of the other minorities. Thus, whilst there are serious doubts as to the strength of identification with their respective groups among second generation Poles and Irish in Britain,[11] the second and third generation Jews have shown signs of somewhat greater persistence of ethnic adherence.[12]

The ethos, or community spirit, of a minority can be narrowed down to certain ultimate objectives, which has led Louis Wirth to propose a fourfold classification. A minority whose main aim is to preserve its own culture and identity and to achieve this in a wider social system based on tolerance and equality of opportunity accorded to all culturally distinct groups, he termed *pluralistic*. One whose aim was to give up its identity and to merge fully with the dominant group to form a homogeneous society, he termed *assimilationist*. A minority who wished to have full political and cultural independence, he termed *secessionist*; whilst one whose aim is to become the dominant group in the society, he called *militant*.[13]

Wirth did recognize that often different sections of a minority are attached to different objectives, but much more important is the fact that the objective that will in the main hold sway over the minority at a particular time will depend not only on the group's own ethos or background but also on the attitude of the dominant group and the status the minority achieves in its social *milieu*. Hence radical changes from one objective to another can take place and such changes must be viewed as the outcome of the interaction between the minority and the dominant society. A few examples may be of interest here. There were definite signs of assimilationist and pluralistic tendencies among East European Jews at the end of the last century. The antagonism of the indigenous population quickly turned this into secessionist aims in the form of Zionism, and into militancy evidenced by the Jewish Socialist and anarchist groups active particularly in the East End of London. The Poles undoubtedly established themselves in post-war Britain with ultimate secessionist objectives to be achieved by a return to Poland. Inability to achieve this aim has created a pluralistic stance. The West Indians, on the other hand, started out with assimilationist aims, but these have been largely frustrated and there are signs of growing militancy in that group.[14]

The upshot is that minority objectives, dominant attitudes and other pertinent factors impinge on one another; their interaction gives rise to a new social situation, a changed social system. The processes thus set in motion have been explained by a number of theories. One of the earliest theories, called 'the race relations cycle', but extended to include all immigrant groups, postulated that minorities pass through several stages: first there is peaceful *contact* with the host society; followed by *competition* for scarce resources, i.e., housing and employment; leading to *conflict*, instanced by discrimination and riots; after a period giving way to *accommodation* between the minority and dominant group, the latter accepting the presence of the minority which in turn learns to fill inferior roles; finally the cycle terminating in *assimilation* which is produced by a thorough mixing between the groups in the biological sense, that is through intermarriage, thus bringing about the disappearance of distinct ethnic sub-communities.[15] This was a neat formulation, but it proved false since it did not accord with the reality as most frequently found in inter-ethnic relations. Most ethnic relations, as exemplified by the British scene and that of other societies, exhibit side by side tendencies to accommodation in some spheres such as employment and conflict in others such as marriage. There has been a good deal of accommodation in the work situation, although even this is far from entirely free of conflict.[16] On the other hand there is ample evidence that there is a great deal of resistance both on the part of the English population and the minority groups such as the Jews, the Indians and the Pakistanis, to inter-marriage.[17] The authors of this theory admitted later that the cycle can regress, in other words that periods of conflict can sometimes erupt after a certain amount of accommodation has taken place. What is more, the final outcome is not always the same. Some minorities in certain situations will tend to-wards assimilation, others will not. And Charles Price points out that assimilation may be uneven within the group itself.[18] Thus, the Jews in England have certainly assimilated as far as language is concerned but not in regard to religion.

Another theory which developed in the United States, re-volving similarly around the idea of eventual assimilation of minorities, was that of the 'melting pot'. This was modified into the 'triple melting pot' to accord with the persisting differen-tiation of American society according to the major religions of Protestantism, Catholicism and Judaism. More recently it has been pointed out that a fourfold division was necessary to separate out the Negroes, whilst some discern a new period emerging 'beyond the melting pot' in which ethnic group differentiation persists along the lines of religion, race and even national origin.[19] The situation in America is indeed unclear. Moreover the theories mentioned have not been very useful in attempts made to explain and clarify the picture. It is no surprise, therefore, to find widely contradictory state-ments: some students of the American scene foresee a possible realignment of group loyalties, where ethnic identity will become a thing of the past and the disintegration of colour lines will take place,[20] whilst others purport to have proved that there are no indications of a substantial progress towards racial amalgamation to occur within the next hundred years or even for a longer period.[21]

Similarly our comparative study of minorities in Britain suggests that there is no simple explanation for the relations between such ethnic groups and the dominant society. Although diachronic comparisons have weaknesses, for we are dealing with minorities in different total social situations, the problems faced by minorities in adjusting to the British conditions appear often to be similar. The chief differences, highlighted by the particular ethos of each group, seem to have stemmed from their backgrounds rather than from the situation in this country. Therefore, although the existence of some unique historical features must be recognized, it is my view that general explanatory theories make sense and would be useful for a proper understanding of the reciprocal influence operating between the internal mechanism of identification (such as we have discussed above) and the nexus and interaction between the minority and the majority. The theories of assimilation expounded above, even if it is accepted that assimilation is a two-way process which affects not only minorities but society as a whole, are of dubious value, as has already been argued. They are certainly far too unsophisticated to be used for explaining what are highly complex situations, which empirically do not seem to lend themselves to analysis by means of their simple conceptual framework.

There are, however, two possible approaches which might pay off in our concluding analysis. One is the theory of pluralistic integration, the other the power-conflict theory. The idea of pluralism is that groups may be found in the same society which, although they may accept and contribute to certain general features of the society of which they are part, nevertheless maintain their own identity. Or as Michael Banton puts it, plural societies are those 'in which there is a common realm of political rights and social valuations together with separate spheres of community living'.[22] In an ideal situation none of the various sub-cultures or sub-communities would dominate over others. But most plural situations are only approximations of such an ideal society; they usually contain elements of both coercion and consensus. Societies containing slavery, colonial societies and those in which legitimized authority is generally sought, all contain the two polar elements but in different degrees. However, in all of them dominant groups will be discernible and therefore R. A. Schermerhorn's definition of integration is apt: 'a process whereby units or elements of a society are brought into an active and co-ordinated compliance with the ongoing activities and object-ives of the dominant group'.[23]

The idea is consequently clearly there that minority groups, as defined above, will occupy subordinate positions *vis-à-vis* the dominant section of society. This section is that 'collect-ivity within society which has pre-eminent authority to func-tion both as guardians and sustainers of the controlling value system, and as prime allocators of rewards in society'.[24] The dominant section may be a restricted *élite*, a governmental apparatus, or a coalition of interest groups; or it may even be viewed as composed of the entire majority population. The minorities in Britain, whether they have an ex-colonial or a European refugee background, have realized that although British society has pluralistic facets, seen in religious toler-ance, to give just one example, on the whole they have to ad-just to an inferior minority status and from this viewpoint the dominant group is the whole of the majority English population.

The status gap can be seen most vividly in the social dis-tance maintained by the English in their relationship with minority groups. The rejection is strongest when it concerns intermarriage. What is highly significant is that the rejection is echoed through the vast majority of the indigenous popula-tion. This statement is not based on the highly selective and probably biased sample of contributors to Enoch Powell's postbag,[25] but on the kind of scientific surveys carried out by M. Tumin and others.[26] In some spheres, such as employment, we have seen that integration is proceeding more success-fully, in that religious affiliation or racial characteristics or nationality and language matter somewhat less. But even here the peculiar employment situations I have described suggest that the integration of minorities represents, overall, a co-ordinated compliance with the objectives of the dominant group. The latter in this context is a coalition of interest groups, i.e. trade unions, employers and established political parties. And although within the coalition itself there are sub-ordinate and dominant groups, that is the working class and the employers, only a crude Marxist theory could equate the indigenous English working class and the various minority groups which have been 'guided' into the lowliest and most underprivileged sectors of the economy, mainly by the instrument of discrimination. Similarly in housing various ethnic groups were seen to have had to contend with those in dominant positions, exemplified in this case by the local government apparatus.

The social distance has been maintained, however, by both sides: the minorities as well as the English. The comments of two members of the Jewish community bring out this point succinctly. One of them was well satisfied with the genuine friendship his Gentile friends displayed towards him in an organization in which he was active. But he objected to the fact that he was regarded by his non-Jewish friends as a kind of *special person*, an ambassador of the Jews. The other case concerns the Jewish man who remarked that he 'went out of his way' to have Gentile neighbours in for tea. This kind of friendship pattern lacks spontaneity in the mixing between Jew and non-Jew.[27] Similarly, and understandably, the majority of Jamaicans, whilst expressing no animosity towards their white neighbours, prefer 'their own kind'.[28] I say *understandably* because by 'their own kind' they specifically mean other Jamaicans and not other West Indians and certainly not simply other coloured people.[29] At a more abstract level we find Polish students, when discussing their naturalization to become British citizens, expressing a strong Polish national consciousness.[30] One can multiply these examples with illustrations from the Irish, Italian and Chinese communities.[31]

Of course social distance may serve to crystallize the identification of minority members with their groups of origin. A statement like Lewis Nkosi's 'I am poor but I'm black, thank God' argues that the social distance imposed between White and Negro is advantageous sometimes for the latter even if only negatively, in the sense that the Negro does not expect too much from English society and hence faces fewer disappointments.[32] An attempt to point to the more positive advantages of 'negritude' and an interest in rediscovering or developing an African Black culture is growing among the West

Indians in England.[33] This is not surprising. Having at the outset adopted the British way of life as their model, the West Indians were rebuffed upon settlement in this country. There was a real possibility here of developing what Stonequist termed a *marginal personality*.[34] The marginal man has to adjust himself to a dual cultural identification which some writers have suggested may lead to a state of social schizophrenia. The modern Jews have been postulated as one of the most vivid examples of a group on the brink of such a state. This, at a time when many of them are less religiously identified, may explain the fervent appeal of Zionism to the great majority of Jews. The Irish too have faced the same problem, which is particularly acute for the second generation who must find their identity from a background of 'the Irish Middle Nation'.[35] Separateness, which manifests itself in residential segregation, in cultural distinctiveness and limited social mixing, tends to solve for minority groups the problems of identity.

With the social distances maintained and the dominant-subordinate pattern of ethnic relations entrenched, one may wonder how well a theory of pluralistic integration really explains processes at work in our society. The question mark attaches in particular to that loosely used term 'integration', unless we reiterate that integration must be understood in the narrower sense in which it was defined above, that is as adjustment to and compliance with the dominant section of society. It will also be observed that within the framework of this theory the notion of assimilation has been avoided. It could be readily argued that the concept of acculturation is more useful here. Whilst assimilation implies changes that bring about the disappearance of the minority group, acculturation is regarded as a process whereby the minority becomes more akin to the dominant group, e.g. in language, dress, etc., although it continues to exist as a separate entity.[36] This certainly accords with the idea of pluralism, and empirical evidence can be adduced from many minorities to show that such a process is in fact operating.[37] Pluralistic integration then does not entail equality in status or opportunities or even legal rights between the sub-communities; it does, however, entail a separate identity for both the dominant and the subordinate groups of society.

The concepts of pluralistic integration and that of assimilation are useful if we wish to *describe* the kind of adjustment that can emerge in a society which has had to contend with inter-ethnic relations. But we thus gain only a *static* picture, for these concepts become ineffective when we wish to uncover the intervening processes – that is the processes at work between the inception of inter-ethnic relations and the eventual, possibly final, adjustment that may be reached. Therefore to see more clearly the *dynamic* aspects involved in the changes and developments of a society which includes minorities we can attempt a brief analysis of the situation in Britain with the aid of the power-conflict theory. This postulates that societies are endemically exposed to conflict situations and power contests between subordinate and dominant groups. Sociologists who have expounded this kind of theory to explain ethnic relations adopt a wider and more complex interpretation of how the social system functions. They do not reject the idea that society is an ongoing system within which the various elements mutually affect each other, in this way contributing to its maintenance and vitality. The maintenance of some kind of system in social relationship does not, however, mean the perpetuation of the *status quo* of a system which develops at a particular point of time.

John Rex put the position of such sociologists very clearly when he says: 'the existence of conflicting group interests does not mean that there is a perpetual war of all against all, or of class against class'. If there were society would cease to exist.

What happens is that 'the various groups mobilize what power they can to enforce compliance with their wishes, but that a point is reached in the power struggle where a realistic adjustment of interests is arrived at, at least temporarily, or organizational means are established for peaceful bargaining about which aims of which group shall be realized'.[38]

Thus an overall social system exists within which conflicts and tensions are managed by various organizational means.

Conflicts are also blurred and modified by various institution-alized aspects of society, such as the existence of status hier-archies and modes of social mobility.

A power-conflict theory need not, therefore, posit limitless conflict and does not imply that we are to 'cast ourselves adrift on a sea of ceaseless flux with only the waves to guide us'.[39] But conflict, even if circumscribed, will be met, and it is carried out by the use of power available to the various con-testing parties. 'Power' is defined by H. M. Blalock as the '*total resources* and the degree to which these resources are *mobilized* in the services of those persons or groups exercising the power'.[40] The resources will include economic means, political rights, education and expertise, and so on. The amount of resources available to a group will not necessarily vary in direct proportion to their numbers.

In the British situation it is obvious that the resources avail-able to the dominant section of the population are far greater than those which any of the ethnic minorities have. It is easy to see, therefore, that the English population is in an advanta-geous position and that they will attempt to maintain their privileges. In real terms this means that some minorities, in this case the more recently settled coloured groups, are kept by the agreement of trade unions and employers in the lowest paid jobs, and they are excluded practically altogether from certain housing facilities.[41] These minorities are in fact those with the least resources available, and hence they are less powerful than some of the other minorities such as the Jews, or the Poles, who are better endowed with resources and their mobilization or utilization. The differences between these minority groups are clearly reflected in the different degrees to which they have experienced social mobility (which I have considered in Chapter 4). There can be no question that social mobility is a central issue and most commentators on ethnic relations in Britain have stressed that the amount of open conflict, as opposed to concealed conflict, is likely to depend primarily on the chances of the underprivileged ethnic minori-ties to better their socio-economic position. There are signs already that these minorities are acquiring somewhat greater resources and particularly a greater ability to mobilize these in their interests. American experience has shown that such modest socio-economic advances have in fact heightened militant attitudes among minorities still grossly deprived. And the emergence of working-class racialism, to which reference is made below, is similarly explained on the grounds that improved conditions of severely deprived minorities threatens the one status dimension where the indigenous groups similarly deprived rank higher – providing the racial factor is regarded as significant. All this suggests that the conflict situation may, therefore, sharpen in the near future.[42]

Now, although I suggested that the theory of pluralistic integration is not as effective as the power-conflict theory in teasing out the dynamic aspects of ethnic relations, this is not to say that these relations are characterized only by conflict. For there are important areas of cooperation, and where conflicting interests do arise violent conflict certainly does not appear to be the most favoured mode of changing the situation and thus resolving the problem. Examples of cooperative efforts would be the inter-ethnic organizations[43] which function to exert influence peacefully in certain situations. Again a good deal of organized opinion within minority communities has favoured peaceful coexistence even where ethnic groups experienced serious frustrations through active discrimination directed against them by the majority.

There are signs, too, that attempts are being made by the dominant section of society to resolve problems in major conflict areas. The Race Relations Act designed to lessen discrimination is just one such step in that direction, however imperfect it may be. The dilemma and contradiction in the situation is that side by side with formal policy oriented towards the managing of tensions there are still the local and more informal means at the disposal of the dominant section to keep minorities in subordinate positions. If the situation is aggravated for some of the groups by the existence of a subtle 'colour line', then more serious opposition may be expected in the future from the most under-privileged coloured minorities.

Does this mean that the wider theoretical framework based on an analysis of power-conflict situations must distinguish between coloured and European minorities? John Rex suggests in fact that, for instance, the Jewish minority occupies a position outside the stratification system whilst coloured groups are beneath it; in other words that there is a generic difference between the social situations of the coloured and white minorities.[44] In terms of definitions one would then have to distinguish sharply between 'ethnic' minorities recognizable by means of religion, language or culture, and 'racial' minorities distinguishable simply in phenotypical terms.[45] If this be so, what is important to discover is whether despite certain similarities between all minority-majority situations differences may nevertheless exist which would suggest the possibility that the destinies of coloured groups would differ radically from those of white minorities.

The kind of crucial question one must pose, therefore, is as follows. It is true that both, say, the Jewish and West Indian immigrant generations have served as pariah and scapegoat groups in British society[46] and that both have produced militant protest movements, but is it likely that the West Indians, like the Jews before them, will proceed to improve their socio-economic position quite substantially and that in the longer run militancy will subside among West Indians as it did among Jews? We need not be detained here by the complex problem of the sense in which there is social mobility for members of minorities. The latter may be forced to stay outside the class, status and power systems of the host society, but in socio-economic terms, measured by such objective criteria as income, occupation and consumption, members of minorities undeniably experience social mobility. In this sense the Jews have risen rapidly within two generations; so have to a lesser degree the post-war Europeans and the Irish. In contrast the Asians and the West Indians have fared rather badly and the indications are that their socio-economic conditions are improving very slowly if at all. Is it that the coloured minorities cannot really break the log-jam simply because of the colour factor? There can be little doubt that there is a certain element of this at play. This was clearly illustrated by the evidence presented above on discrimination against coloured immigrants (pp. 91, 104.). Yet severe discrimination against

Jews which was rampant a few decades ago did not prevent the latter from raising their socio-economic standard from the depth of poverty. Consequently, one would suspect that there is another factor at work.

The material adduced in previous chapters and its analysis suggest quite clearly that this other determining factor in socio-economic advancement is the degree of urbanism with which minority groups are endowed. 'Urbanism' would in this sense be defined as the possession of certain skills and attitudes which are particularly necessary and favourable for life in an urban-industrial society.[47] This means that in a widely defined power-conflict[48] situation sheer militancy will not achieve what better education, occupational skills and flexibility in adjusting to changed conditions can achieve for minority individuals.

There is the example of the Kenya Asians in Britain. This group has an urban background with an occupational distribution biased towards the upper reaches of the socio-economic scale[49] and is characterized by a decidedly middle class attitude. At the same time it has been subject to discrimination on account of colour which has caused in the first instance large numbers to become *déclassés*. Despite this, the early indications are that they have not adopted a militant stance and have in a short space of time been able to move outwards to the suburbs and upwards in terms of social mobility.[50]

A strikingly similar situation obtains among a group of fairly recent Oriental Jewish immigrants. This group, too, was an urbanized one, but suffered not only from problems of adjustment but also experienced in some instances discrimination on account of colour as well as on account of their being Jewish. The group is nevertheless well set on an upwardly mobile course no different from earlier European Jewish immigrants. This has been facilitated by an adaptability and versatility gained in prior urban experience and the possession of certain skills and attitudes useful in an industrial-urban environment.[51]

These examples do not deny the existence of power-conflict situations where inter-ethnic relations are based on a minority versus dominant-group pattern. They do show, however, that the conflict may be more successfully waged by those minorities whose power is based on greater resources consisting of educational, occupational and social adaptability skills. It may be a matter of debate whether in the case of some minorities, such as the West Indians and the Pakistanis, who possess such resources to a much lower degree, a militant attitude may be the necessary catalyst in a process which would then lead to the acquisition of such resources. To put it bluntly, it is not at all clear that Black Power activities will induce the dominant group to provide, for instance, better educational facilities. These may in fact produce the opposite effect through a 'white backlash'. At the same time one cannot but recognize that so long as such minorities are kept deprived of resources to enable them to compete more fairly with other groups in Britain and so long as they are victimized on account of their colour, a Black Power movement will exist. This can be seen as a symptom that something is wrong with our society.[52]

However, the critical groups of Kenya Asians and Oriental Jews could possibly point to the thesis that colour alone need not prevent socio-economic advancement and that militancy may be absent where the minority possesses other resources with which it can take up the struggle. But supposing that social mobility increases for the most underprivileged minorities. This will not *ipso facto* do away with ethnic differentiation, prejudice and social distance. In an American study by Robin Williams it was found that more low status people expressed distance towards Negroes and more high status people towards Jews. It was suggested that 'each category was responding to the group which represented the most actual threat to its own privileges'.[53] The situation may be similar in this country. Whilst dockers march against accepting more coloured workers, antagonism shown by conservative business elements towards some Jewish tycoons is, as Chaim Bermant says, 'a polite, or not so polite, expression of anti-semitism'.[54] These are undoubtedly expressions of negative reference group behaviour. The positive comparisons that a status-group of the English population will make, will be with other status groups within that majority. Those sociologists who have drawn attention to 'the paradox of the coexistence of gross inequality with a high degree of political consensus'[55] do not in any way throw light on ethnic relations. The consensus operates *within* the dominant majority, to the exclusion, even if only partial exclusion, of ethnic minorities.

It is of paramount importance, therefore, that different stratification orders should not be confounded. The class divisions of modern Britain are cut right across by ethnic divisions. Societies must be seen as capable of carrying dual or multiple stratification systems.[56] The processes within these systems may be analysed by the same kind of theory, using, say, the power-conflict perspective. The outcome of the pressures and relations between different groups within each system may, however, be different. It appears that pressures from below, towards greater equality, have been resolved with less recourse to open conflict, where these pressures have been exerted in post-war Britain by the English working-class. The question is whether the conflicts ensuing in the arena of inter-ethnic relations will be similarly resolved. Two social scientists writing in the 1950s about minorities in the New World concluded pragmatically that it was reasonable to ask that 'we learn how to regulate the conflict arising out of different social and cultural groups in our societies, while allowing them the freedom to struggle for a more equal share in our democratic system'.[57] Is it likely that by the 1970s, we in the Old World will have learned, through the experience of others and our own, how to harness our energies towards the creation of a fully democratic society, where certain ethnic connotations, whether racial, religious, national or cultural, cease to function as the criteria for economic disadvantage or social stigma?

Notes and Bibliographies

CHAPTER 1

1 Louis Wirth, *Community Life and Social Policy*, University of Chicago Press, 1956, p. 237.

2 R. Glass, 'Insiders – Outsiders' in *Transactions of the Fifth World Congress of Sociology 1962*, International Sociological Association, 1964, pp. 141 f.

3 *Second Report by Commonwealth Immigrants Advisory Council*, Cmnd 2266, HMSO, February 1964, p. 4, and *Third Report by Commonwealth Immigrants Advisory Council*, Cmnd 2458, HMSO, September 1964, p. 3.

4 Britain, with the agreement of Turkey, in fact took over the administration of the island in 1878.

5 Robin Oakley, ed., *New Backgrounds*, Oxford University Press for the Institute of Race Relations (hereafter cited as IRR), 1968, p. 24.

6 Elspeth Huxley, *Back Street New Worlds*, Chatto and Windus, 1964.

7 Oakley, op. cit., p. 25.

8 ibid., p. 40.

9 For further details see Richard Hooper, ed., *Colour in Britain*, British Broadcasting Corporation, 1965, pp. 28, 29.

10 M. Banton, *Race Relations*, Tavistock Publications, 1967, p. 102.

11 ibid.

12 Hooper, op. cit., p. 30.

13 See Douglas Manley, 'The West Indian Background' in S. K. Ruck, ed., *The West Indian Comes to England*, Routledge, 1960, pp. 3–8.

14 See Katrin FitzHerbert, 'The West Indian Background' in Oakley, op. cit., p. 2.

15 E. Franklin Frazier, *The Negro Family in the United States*, University of Chicago Press, Chicago, 1966.

16 M. S. Elkins, *Slavery*, Grosset and Dunlop, New York, 1963.

17 FitzHerbert, op. cit., p. 15.

18 Sheila Patterson, *Dark Strangers*, Tavistock, 1963, p. 7.

19 Malcolm Calley, 'West Indian Churches in England' in *New Society*, 6 August 1964, p. 15.

20 FitzHerbert, op. cit., p. 17.

21 Douglas Manley, op. cit., p. 40.

22 Hooper, op. cit., p. 31.

23 Michael Banton, *White and Coloured*, Jonathan Cape, 1959, p. 125.

24 Judith Henderson, Part II, 'A Sociological Report' in J. A. G. Griffith *et al.*, *Coloured Immigrants in Britain*, OUP for IRR, 1960, p. 83.

25 Michael Banton, op. cit., p. 55 f.

26 Anthony H. Richmond, *The Colour Problem*, Penguin, 1961, p. 235.

27 Judith Henderson, op. cit., p. 51.

28 Hooper, op. cit., p. 35.

29 Africanization means for instance that in certain public services in which many Indians, mainly Sikhs, have been employed, these are being replaced by African nationals.

30 Hooper, op. cit., p. 35.

31 T. Zinkin, *Caste Today*, OUP, 1962.

32 Roger T. Bell, 'The Indian Background' in Oakley, op. cit., p. 54.

33 M. N. Srinivas, *Caste in Modern India*, Asia Publishing House, London, 1962.

34 Roger T. Bell, op. cit., p. 64 and Hooper, op. cit., pp. 36, 41.

35 Hooper, ibid.

36 Ng Kwee Choo, *The Chinese in London*, OUP for IRR, 1968, p. 3.

37 ibid., p. 22.

38 Ta Chen, *Emigrant Communities in South China*, OUP, 1939.

39 Ng Kwee Choo, op. cit., pp. 24, 66.

40 John A. Jackson, 'The Irish' in Ruth Glass *et al.*, *London*, MacGibbon & Kee, 1964, p. 293.

41 A particularly interesting anthropological feature of the Irish

people is the combination of light coloured eyes and dark hair. According to the *Encyclopaedia Britannica* 40 per cent have blue eyes, whilst most have dark brown (not black) hair.

42 See Paul Foot, *Immigration and Race in British Politics*, Penguin, 1965, p. 81.

43 J. A. Jackson, *The Irish in Britain*, Routledge, 1963, p. 2.

44 ibid., p. 4.

45 John Rex and Robert Moore, *Race, Community and Conflict*, OUP/IRR, 1967, p. 85.

46 C. Arensberg and S. T. Kimball, *Family and Community in Ireland*, Cambridge, Mass., 1940.

47 J. A. Jackson, op. cit., pp. 32, 69.

48 James Parkes, 'The History of the Anglo-Jewish Community' in Maurice Freedman, ed., *A Minority in Britain*, Vallentine-Mitchell, 1955, pp. 5–8.

49 Cecil Roth, 'The Resettlement of the Jews in England in 1656' in V. D. Lipman, ed., *Three Centuries of Anglo–Jewish History*, Heffer/Jewish Historical Society, Cambridge, 1961, p. 2.

50 In Tsarist Russia Jews were not allowed to live in the larger towns.

51 A. Antonovski and E. Tcherikower, *The Early Jewish Labor Movement in the United States*, Yivo, New York, 1961.

52 Ernest Krausz, *Leeds Jewry: its History and Social Structure*, Heffer/Jewish Historical Society, Cambridge, 1964, p. 4.

53 Lloyd P. Gartner, *The Jewish Immigrant in England 1870–1914*, Allen & Unwin, 1959.

54 Francesca M. Wilson, *They Came as Strangers*, Hamish Hamilton, 1959, p. 233.

55 Jerzy Zubrzycki, *Polish Immigrants in Britain*, Nijhoff, The Hague, 1956.

56 See *Planning – British Immigration Policy*, a broadsheet issued by Political and Economic Planning (hereafter cited as PEP) Vol. XIV, No. 268, July 1947.

57 Francesca M. Wilson, op. cit., p. 237.

58 See *Planning – British Immigration Policy*, op. cit., p. 18.

59 J. A. Jackson, *The Irish in Britain*, op. cit., p. 24.

60 Ceri Peach, *West Indian Migration to Britain*, OUP/IRR, p. xii.

61   Christopher Bagley, 'Immigrant Minorities in the Nether-
      lands', a background paper from the Institute of Race Rela-
      tions Conference held at the University of Aston in Birming-
      ham, 18–19 September 1969.
62   Ceri Peach, op. cit., pp. xiii–xiv.
63   Charles A. Price, *Jewish Settlers in Australia*, Social Science
      Monograph No. 23, The Australian National University,
      1964, p. 21.
64   Anthony H. Richmond, 'Colored Colonials in the United
      Kingdom' in A. M. and C. B. Rose, *Minority Problems*,
      New York, Harper and Row, 1965, p. 77.
65   Ernest Krausz, *Leeds Jewry*, op. cit., p. 4.
66   J. A. Jackson, *The Irish in Britain*, op. cit., p. 29.
67   Katrin FitzHerbert, 'The West Indian Background', op. cit.,
      p. 4.

Bibliography

Louis Wirth, *Community Life and Social Policy*, University of
    Chicago Press, 1956.
M. Banton, *Race Relations*, Tavistock, 1967.
Richard Hooper, ed., *Colour in Britain*, BBC Publications, 1965.
Robin Oakley, ed., *New Backgrounds*, OUP/IRR, 1968.
S. K. Ruck, ed., *The West Indian Comes to England*, Routledge,
    1960.
Sheila Patterson, *Dark Strangers*, Tavistock, 1963.
M. Banton, *White and Coloured*, Jonathan Cape, 1959.
J. A. G. Griffith, *et al.*, *Coloured Immigrants in Britain*, OUP/IRR,
    1960.
A. H. Richmond, *The Colour Problem*, Penguin, 1961.
Ruth Glass *et al.*, *London*, MacGibbon & Kee, 1964.
J. A. Jackson, *The Irish in Britain*, Routledge, 1963.
Paul Foot, *Immigration and Race in British Politics*, Penguin, 1965.
J. Rex and R. Moore, *Race, Community and Conflict*, OUP/IRR,
    1967.
M. Freedman, ed., *A Minority in Britain*, Vallentine Mitchell, 1955.
S. J. Gould and S. Esh, eds., *Jewish Life in Modern Britain*,
    Routledge, 1964.

V. D. Lipman, *Social History of the Jews in England 1850–1950*, Watts, 1954.

Lloyd Gartner, *The Jewish Immigrant in England 1870–1914*, Allen & Unwin, 1959.

Ernest Krausz, *Leeds Jewry: Its History and Social Structure*, Heffers, Cambridge, 1964.

Francesca M. Wilson, *They Came as Strangers*, Hamish Hamilton, 1959.

Jerzy Zubrzycki, *Polish Immigrants in Britain*, Nijhoff, The Hague, 1956.

CHAPTER 2

1 See: *1966 Sample Census*; P. N. Jones, *The Segregation of Immigrant Communities in the City of Birmingham*, University of Hull Publications, 1967, p. 29; J. A. Jackson, *The Irish in Britain*, Routledge 1963, p. 15.

2 See: S. J. Prais and Marlena Schmool, 'The Size and Structure of the Anglo-Jewish Population 1960–1965' in the *Jewish Journal of Sociology*, Vol. X, No. 1, June 1968.

3 E. J. B. Rose, *et al.*, *Colour and Citizenship*, OUP/IRR, 1969, p. 99.

4 ibid. p. 1. By mid-1969 it was suggested that the figure was over 1,200,000 – see *The Times*, 18 June 1969, p. 2.

5 See Zubrzycki, op. cit., p. 63.

6 See Robin Oakley, op. cit., p. 23.

7 See Francesca Wilson, op. cit.

8 PEP *Refugees in Britain*, Vol. XXIV, No. 419, Planning, 17 Feb. 1958, p. 22.

9 See Summary Tables, *1966 Sample Census*, HMSO, 1967, p. 29.

10 See above Chapter 1, p. 10.

11 For the Irish figures see: 'Miscellany' in the *Guardian*, 30.12. 69. This estimate comes from Irish journalists and although it cannot be verified by exact statistics, considering the number of Irish-born people and the constant influx from Ireland the figure is not likely to be an exaggeration.

12 See J. A. Jackson, 'The Irish' in *London*, ed. by Centre for Urban Studies, MacGibbon & Kee, 1964, p. 296. It is worth

noting that proportionately the Irish immigration to Scotland has been even heavier.

13 See V. D. Lipman, *Social History of the Jews in England 1850–1950*, Watts, 1954, pp. 103, 167.

14 See Francesca M. Wilson, *They Came as Strangers*, Hamish Hamilton 1959, pp. 233–7.

15 See David Eversley and Fred Sukdeo, *The Dependants of the Coloured Commonwealth Population of England & Wales*, IRR, 1969, pp. 8, 18.

16 See *Sample Census 1966*, Great Britain-Summary Tables, HMSO, 1967, Table 1.

17 Ceri Peach, *West Indian Migration to Britain – A Social Geography*, OUP/IRR, 1968, p. 76.

18 ibid.

19 E. J. B. Rose, *et al.*, op. cit., p. 100.

20 ibid, p. 102.

21 Ruth Glass and John Westergaard, *London's Housing Needs*, Centre for Urban Studies, 1965; Ceri Peach, op. cit., p. 87.

22 J. A. Jackson, 'The Irish'. op. cit., pp. 301 f; P. N. Jones, op. cit., p. 29; *Race Today*, Dec. 1969, p. 231. There are supposed to be half a million Irish in London, nearly as many as in Dublin – see the *Evening Standard*, 18.8.69.

23 Elspeth Huxley, *Back Street New Worlds*, Chatto & Windus, 1964, pp. 31 f.

24 J. Zubrzycki, *Polish Immigrants in Britain*, Nijhoff, The Hague 1956, pp. 68 f.

25 Huxley, op. cit., p. 69.

26 *Race Today*, Dec. 1969, p. 228; Ng Kwee Choo, *The Chinese in London* IRR/OUP, 1968, pp. 2 f; Anna Craven, *West Africans in London*, IRR, 1969; Studies on Immigration from the Commonwealth, *The Immigrant Communities 2*, The Economist Intelligence Unit, London; V. George and G. Millerson, 'The Cypriot Community in London' in *Race*, Vol. VIII, No. 3, Jan. 1967.

27 See *The Jewish Year Book*, 1967; Gould & Esh, eds, op. cit; E. Krausz, 'Occupation and Social Advancement in Anglo-Jewry' and 'The Edgware Survey: Demographic Results' in the *Jewish Journal of Sociology*, Vols. IV, No. 1 and X, No. 1.

28 See Joe Doherty, 'The Distribution and Concentration of Immigrants in London' in *Race Today*, Dec. 1968, p. 228.

29 Eversley and Sukdeo, op. cit.

30 Peach, op. cit., p. 91; E. J. B. Rose, *et al.*, p. 103.

31 *Race Today*, Dec. 1969, pp. 228–31.

32 P. N. Jones, op. cit., pp. 5, 13.

33 ibid.

34 E. J. B. Rose, *et al.*, op. cit., p. 102.

35 Ruth Glass, *Newcomers: West Indians in London*, Allen & Unwin: Centre for Urban Studies, 1960, p. 41. A 'ghetto' has been defined by the Kerner Commission as an area 'within a city characterized by poverty and acute social disorganization, and inhabited by members of a racial or ethnic group under conditions of involuntary segregation' – quoted in *Race Today*, Dec. 1969, p. 231. For another definition of 'ghetto' see below, p. 159

36 It may be noted that Jews are not included in this and some other statistical tables. This is due to the great difficulty of locating them statistically. For a discussion of this problem see E. Krausz, 'Locating Minority Populations: A Research Problem', in *Race*, X, 3 (1969).

37 Joe Doherty, op. cit.

38 P. N. Jones, op. cit., p. 32.

39 Ceri Peach, op. cit., p. 82.

40 This follows, in a modified form, the model of E. W. Burgess – see R. E. Park, E. W. Burgess and R. D. McKenzie, *The City*, University of Chicago Press, Chicago, 1967.

41 *The Immigrant Communities 2*, op. cit., p. 9.

42 V. D. Lipman, *Social History of the Jews in England 1850–1950*, Watts, 1954, p. 93.

43 E. Krausz, *Leeds Jewry: Its History and Social Structure*, Heffers, Cambridge, 1964, p. 4.

44 E. Krausz, 'The Edgware Survey: Demographic Results' in the *Jewish Journal of Sociology*, Vol. X, No. 1, p. 86.

45 H. Neustatter in M. Freedman, ed., *A Minority in Britain*, Vallentine-Mitchell, 1955, p. 69.

46 E. Krausz, 'The Edgware Survey: Demographic Results', op. cit., p. 95.

47 J. A. Jackson, 'The Irish' in *London*, op. cit., p. 303.

48 J. A. Jackson, *The Irish in Britain*, Routledge, 1963, p. 18.
49 J. A. H. Waterhouse and D. H. Brabban, 'Inquiry into the fertility of Immigrants: Preliminary Report' in *Eugenics Review*, Vol. 56, No. 1, April 1964.
50 See E. J. B. Rose *et al.*, op. cit., p. 104.
51 ibid., pp. 112 f.
52 J. Zubrzycki, op. cit., p. 63.
53 V. George and G. Millerson, op. cit., pp. 279 f.
54 See Ng Kwee Choo, *The Chinese in London*, IRR/OUP, 1968, p. 8. For some data on West Africans see Anna Craven, *West Africans in London*, IRR, 1969.
55 The statistics for the general population usually include the minorities, which means that the special features of the latter will affect the general figures. But since the minorities make up a very small proportion of the total population comparability still remains meaningful.
56 See IRR Facts Paper, *Colour and Immigration in the United Kingdom*, 1969, p. 35.
57 See the *Guardian*, 13 Nov. 1969.
58 It may be noted that the 12% includes 2·8% of births to mothers from other countries, particularly Europe and the United States. See the Registrar General's *Quarterly Return*, Sept. 1969, No. 483, HMSO.
59 E. J. B. Rose, *et al.*, op. cit., p. 118.
60 Ernest Krausz, *Sociology in Britain – A Survey of Research*, Batsford, 1969, pp. 121 f.
61 E. J. B. Rose, *et al.*, op. cit., p. 640.
62 ibid., p. 638.
63 ibid., p. 637.
64 Waterhouse and Brabban, op. cit.
65 A. M. Carr-Saunders, D. C. Jones and C. A. Moser, *Social Conditions in England and Wales*, The Clarendon Press, Oxford, 1958, p. 23.
66 E. Krausz, 'The Edgware Survey: Demographic Results', op. cit., p. 94.
67 Griselda Rowntree and Rachel M. Pierce, 'Birth Control in Britain' in *Population Studies*, July 1961 and November 1961.
68 E. J. B. Rose, *et. al.*, op. cit., p. 115.

69 *Colour and Immigration in the United Kingdom 1968*, IRR
    Facts Paper, p. 10.
70 D. Eversley and F. Sukdeo, *The Dependants of the Coloured
    Commonwealth Population of England and Wales*, IRR, 1969,
    p. 56.
71 See Home Office figures quoted in *Race Today*, Dec. 1969,
    p. viii.
72 See report of announcement made by the Home Secretary in
    the House of Commons on 14 May 1970 – the *Guardian*,
    15.5.70.
73 Eversley and Sukdeo, op. cit., p. 59. See also B. A. Chansar-
    kar, 'Professional Immigrants – Do They Move On?' in
    Race Today, Jan. 1970.
74 E. J. B. Rose, *et al.*, op. cit., p. 637.
75 Institute of Race Relations Facts Paper, *Colour and Immigra-
    tion in the United Kingdom*, 1969, pp. 36 f.; Economist Intel-
    ligence Unit, *Commonwealth Immigration*, June 1967, p. 30.
76 R. K. Kelsall, *Population*, Longman, 1967, p. 72.
77 See K. Jones and A. D. Smith, *The Economic Impact of
    Commonwealth Immigration* (Occasional Papers XXIV),
    Cambridge University Press for The National Institute of
    Economic and Social Research, 1970.
78 Net immigration from Eire has been put at 30,000 per year.
    See R. K. Kelsall, op. cit.
79 See: M. Freedman ed., *A Minority in Britain*, Vallentine Mit-
    chell, 1955; S. J. Prais and Marlena Schmool, 'The Size and
    Structure of the Anglo-Jewish Population 1960–1965' in
    The Jewish Journal of Sociology, Vol. X. No. 1, June 1968.
80 J. Zubrzycki, op. cit., p. 62.

It is evident from this chapter that statistical data for minority
groups are generally scanty and that the details available and their
reliability vary a good deal as between different aspects and groups.
For readers who wish to follow the trends, particularly concerning
the newer immigrants, a few of the more important official sources
are given below. These indicate for instance the kind of statistics
that are made available through Censuses. A few examples are also
given of compilations and analyses carried out by social scientists.

Bibliography

General Register Office, *Census 1961 England and Wales: Birth-place and Nationality Tables*, HMSO, 1964.

General Register Office, *Census 1961 England and Wales: Commonwealth Immigrants in the Conurbations*, HMSO, 1965.

General Register Office, *Census 1961 England and Wales: County Report, London*, HMSO, 1963.

General Register Office, *Census 1961 England and Wales: Fertility Tables* (see Table 20), HMSO, 1966.

General Register Office, *Sample Census 1966 Great Britain: Commonwealth Immigrants Tables*, HMSO, 1969.

General Register Office, *The Registrar General's Statistical Review of England and Wales for the year 1966: Part III Commentary* HMSO, 1970.

Commonwealth Immigrants Act 1962, *Control of Immigration Statistics*, HMSO, London (annual).

Home Office, *Statistics of Foreigners Entering and Leaving the United Kingdom*, HMSO, London (annual).

Institute of Race Relations, *Facts Paper – Colour and Immigration in the United Kingdom* 1969.

Institute of Race Relations, *Facts Paper on the United Kingdom* 1970–71.

Race Today (Statistics Section), published monthly by the Institute of Race Relations, London.

Race Relations Bulletin, published monthly by the Runnymede Trust.

E. J. B. Rose, *et al.*, *Colour and Citizenship*, OUP/IRR, 1969.

Clifford Hill, *Immigration and Integration*, Pergamon, 1970.

CHAPTER 3

1 Paul Foot quotes this figure from the 1949 Royal Commission on Population in his book *Immigration and Race in British Politics*, Penguin, 1965, p. 80.
2 See quote in Michael Banton, *White and Coloured*, Jonathan Cape 1959, p. 55.
3 Paul Foot, op. cit., p. 82.
4 ibid., See Friedrich Engels, *The Conditions of the Working Class in England*, Basil Blackwell, Oxford, 1958, p. 106.

5 ibid., p. 81.

6 See Lloyd P. Gartner, *The Jewish Immigrant in England 1870–1914*, Allen & Unwin, 1959, p. 275.

7 *Charles Booth's London*, selected and edited by A. Fried and R. M. Elman, Hutchinson, 1969, p. 155.

8 Paul Foot, op. cit., p. 87.

9 V. D. Lipman, *Social History of the Jews in England 1850–1950*, Watts, 1954, p. 135.

10 ibid., p. 136.

11 ibid., p. 141.

12 Paul Foot, op. cit., p. 83.

13 Ernest Krausz, *Leeds Jewry: Its History and Social Structure*, Heffer, Cambridge, 1964, p. 21.

14 Kenneth L. Little, 'Race and Society' in *The Race Question in Modern Science*, UNESCO, Paris 1959, p. 195.

15 K. L. Little, *Negroes in Britain*, Kegan Paul, 1948, p. 57.

16 ibid., p. 197.

17 ibid., pp. 199, 200

18 W. W. Daniel, *Racial Discrimination in England*, Penguin Books, 1968, p. 201.

19 ibid., p. 155.

20 See Henri Tajfel in Richard Hooper, ed. *Colour in Britain*, op. cit., p. 129.

21 J. Zubrzycki, *Polish Immigrants in Britain*, op. cit., p. 85.

22 Clifford S. Hill, *How Colour Prejudiced is Britain?* Gollancz, 1965, p. 38.

23 ibid., p. 32.

24 See A. N. Oppenheimer, *Questionnaire Design and Attitude Measurement*, Heinemann, 1966, p. 124.

25 See H. Otto Dahlke, 'Social Distance' in J. Gould and W. L. Kolb, eds., *A Dictionary of the Social Sciences*, Tavistock, 1964, pp. 653–4.

26 Nicholas Deakin, 'Race, The Politicians and Public Opinion', mimeographed BSA 1969 Race Relations Conference paper, pp. 9, 10. See also below, pp. 130 f.

27 Michael Banton, *White and Coloured*, Jonathan Cape, 1959, p. 210.

28 ibid., pp. 200–2.

29 Clifford S. Hill, op. cit., p. 34.

30 ibid., p. 36.
31 ibid., p. 45.
32 E. J. B. Rose and associates, *Colour and Citizenship*, OUP/ IRR, 1969, p. 598.
33 ibid., p. 553.
34 ibid., p. 596
35 Reproduced from E. J. B. Rose, *et al.*, op. cit., p. 593; see also Ruth Glass, *Newcomers: West Indians in London*, Allen & Unwin for Centre for Urban Studies, 1960.
36 Danny Lawrence, 'How Prejudiced are We?' in *Race Today*, Vol. 1, No. 6, Oct. 1969, pp. 174 f.
37 E. J. B. Rose, *et al.*, op. cit., p. 598.
38 I know this personally from relatives and friends who have experienced such hospitality.
39 See M. Banton in Richard Hooper, ed., *Colour in Britain*, op. cit., p. 125.
40 See Michael Wallach, 'Marrying Out' in the *Jewish Chronicle*, 23 May 1969, p. 7.
41 See Dorothy Kuya, 'Mixed Marriages and the Problems the Children Face', unpublished monograph, IRR Library, 1967, Preface, p. 1.
42 See Max Beloff, *Britain's Liberal Empire 1897–1921 – Imperial Sunset Vol. 1*, Methuen, 1969.
43 Paul Foot, *Immigration and Race in British Politics*, Penguin, 1965, pp. 95–6.
44 ibid., p. 106.
45 Andrew Sharf, *The British Press and Jews under Nazi Rule*, OUP, 1964, p. 171.
46 J. Zubrzycki, *Polish Immigrants in Britain*, Nijhoff, 1956, pp. 81, 82.
47 Paul Foot, op. cit., p. 119.
48 ibid., p. 118.
49 Quoted in J. A. Jackson, *The Irish in Britain*, op. cit., p. 155.
50 See Norman Cohn, *Warrant for Genocide*, Eyre & Spottiswoode, 1967, p. 152.
51 Andrew Sharf, *The British Press and Jews under Nazi Rule*, OUP, 1964, p. 170.
52 ibid., p. 206.

53 See Paul Foot, op. cit., p. 176 and Nicholas Deakin, 'The Politics of the Commonwealth Immigrants Bill' in the *Political Quarterly*, Vol. 39, No. 1. Jan–March 1968.

54 Nicholas Deakin, ed., *Colour and the British Electorate*, Pall Mall Press, 1965, p. 158.

55 Sheila Patterson, *Immigration and Race Relations in Britain 1960–67*, OUP 1969, p. 36.

56 See Walter Adams, 'The Refugee Scholars of the 1930s' in the *Political Quarterly*, op. cit.

57 See Paul Foot, op. cit., p. 120.

58 Nicholas Deakin, 'The Politics of the Commonwealth Immigrants Bill', op. cit., p. 35.

59 Richard Hooper, ed., *Colour in Britain*, op. cit., Ch. 13 and p. 231.

60 S. K. Rusk ed., *The West Indian Comes to England*, op. cit., Part 3.

61 Peter Calvocoressi, 'The Official Structure of Conciliation' in the *Political Quarterly*, Vol. 39, No. 1, Jan.–March 1968, p. 52.

62 Paul Foot, op. cit., p. 226.

63 Michael Banton, *White and Coloured*, op. cit., pp. 121 f.

64 Clifford S. Hill and David Mathews, eds., *Race – A Christian Symposium*, Victor Gollancz, 1968, p. 183.

65 Richard Hooper, ed., *Colour in Britain*, op. cit., p. 181; at the time of the Notting Hill riots the British Council of Churches declared: 'We are shocked by the evidence of colour prejudice as one of the causes of recent disturbances involving coloured people in Great Britain'. They also stated: 'The Churches could not consent to limitation of immigration on grounds of colour.' Quoted in J. A. G. Griffith, ed., *Coloured Immigrants in Britain*. op. cit., p. 149.

66 For many examples see Hooper, ed., op. cit., pp. 185–7.

67 J. Zubrzycki, op. cit., p. 82.

68 J. A. Jackson, *The Irish in Britain*, op. cit., pp. 154 f.

69 Quoted in J. A. Jackson, op. cit., p. 157. See also, G. Scott, *The Roman Catholics*, Hutchinson, 1967.

70 J. A. Jackson, ibid.

71 V. George and G. Millerson, 'The Cypriot Community in London' in *Race*, Vol. VIII, No. 3, Jan. 1967, p. 20.

72 James Parkes, *Antisemitism*, Vallentine-Mitchell, 1963, p. 176.

73 George Thayer, *The British Political Fringe*, Anthony Blond, 1968, Ch. 1.

74 See the *Guardian*, 17 June, 1969, p. 4.

75 Thayer, op. cit., p. 21. See also: Ian Henderson 'All's now quiet on the National Front' in *New World*, the UNA monthly, July 1970.

76 Paul Foot, op. cit., p. 209.

77 J. Zubrzycki, op. cit., p. 84.

78 Quoted in J. A. G. Griffith, ed., op. cit., p. 79.

79 G. E. Simpson and J. M. Yinger, *Racial and Cultural Minorities*, New York, Harper & Row, 3rd edn., 1965, p. 159.

80 S. Collins, *Coloured Minorities in Britain*, Lutterworth, 1959, p. 138.

81 Ng Kwee Choo, *The Chinese in London*, OUP, 1968, p. 49.

82 Hugh Harris ed. *The Jewish Year Book*, 1967, p. 48.

83 ibid., p. 55.

84 Ernest Krausz, *Leeds Jewry*, op. cit., p. 65.

85 R. Desai, *Indian Immigrants in Britain*, OUP/IRR, 1963, p. 104.

86 Mary Grigg, *The White Question*, Secker & Warburg, 1967, p. 149.

87 Lloyd P. Gartner, *The Jewish Immigrant in England, 1870–1914*, Allen & Unwin, 1959, pp. 100 f.

88 Quoted in Gartner, ibid., pp. 109 f.

89 Quoted, ibid., p. 127.

90 ibid., p. 266.

91 Quoted in J. A. Jackson, *The Irish in Britain*, op. cit., p. 122.

92 ibid., pp. 124–5.

93 ibid p. 125. Manifestations of this came to the surface again at the time of the disturbances in Northern Ireland in the summer of 1969. This was clearly reflected in Press reports. See for instance the *Evening Standard*, 14.8.69, p. 17; and John O'Callaghan in the *Guardian*, 18.8.69.

94 Judith Henderson, 'Race Relations in Britain', in J. A. G. Griffith, *et al.*, op. cit., p. 87.

95 See Mary Grigg, *The White Question*, op. cit., p. 116.

96 W. E. B. du Bois, *Black Reconstruction*, Harcourt, New York, 1935.

97 A. Sivanandan, 'A Farewell to Liberalism' in *News Letter*, IRR April 1969, pp. 176–8.

98 See Mary Grigg, op. cit., p. 116.

99 C. Karadia, 'The Black Peoples' Alliance' in *News Letter*, IRR, June 1968, p. 231.

100 See the *Guardian*, 27.4.70.

101 See John Rex, 'Economic Aspects of Racism and Race Prejudice and the Urban Crisis', UNESCO, 1969.

102 Philip Mason, 'Regionalism, Black Power, and the Revolt of Youth' in *Race Today*, Vol. 1, No. 2, June 1969, p. 46. See for instance references to more recent Black Power demonstrations e.g. in Brixton in August 1969, quoted in *Race Today*, Vol. 1, No. 5, Sept 1969, p. iii of Commentary Section.

103 See J. A. G. Griffith *Coloured Immigrants in Britain*, op. cit., Part IV on legal aspects of immigration.

104 Facts Paper – *Colour and Immigration in the United Kingdom 1969*, IRR Second Edition 1969, pp. 12 f.

105 E. J. B. Rose and associates, *Colour and Citizenship*, OUP for IRR, 1969, p. 54.

106 David Steel, *No Entry*, C. Hurst, 1969, p. 219. The author says that some of these immigrants have secured lowly paid jobs and have not been able to bring over their families.

107 Jews and other European immigrants were often treated as 'stateless' after the Second World War even if allowed to settle in Britain.

108 See *The Race Relations Act 1968*, HMSO 1968; and Ian A. Macdonald, *Race Relations and Immigration Law*, Butterworth, 1969, especially pp. 90, 97 and 120.

109 Frank Cousins, 'Some Thoughts on Community Relations', *Race Today*, August 1969, p. 104. It may be noted here that the Community Relations Committee took over from the National Committee for Commonwealth Immigrants – see also above, pp. 66 f.

110 See *Race Today*, July 1969, Commentary, p. iii.

111 Louis J. Ellman, 'The Fforde Greene Affair' in *Race Today*, Sept. 1969, pp. 153 f.

112 See these views expressed by Jocelyn Barrow in the *Guardian*, 11.12.69, p. 22.

113 See the *Sunday Times*, 2 November 1969.

114 Mrs Ann Dummett quoted in *News Letter*, IRR, April 1969, p. 155.

115 *The Times*, 24 October 1969.

116 The magnitude of the influx of dependants was considered in the last chapter.

117 Bob Hepple, *Race, Jobs and the Law in Britain*, Allen Lane, The Penguin Press 1968, p. 92.

118 See *Patterns of Prejudice*, Institute of Jewish Affairs, London, Vol. 1, No. 1, Jan.-Feb. 1967, p. 28.

119 E. J. B. Rose and associates, op. cit., pp. 678 f.

120 See the *Jewish Chronicle*, July 18, 1969, p. 6.

121 Gordon W. Allport, *The Nature of Prejudice*, Doubleday, New York, Anchor Books edition, 1958, p. 8.

122 Morris Ginsberg, 'On Prejudice' in The *Jewish Journal of Sociology*, Vol. 1, No. 1. April, 1959, p. 120.

123 Michael Banton, *Race Relations*, Tavistock 1967, p. 298; see also: H. J. Eysenck, *Uses and Abuses of Psychology*, Penguin, 1962, Chapter 14, and Allport, op. cit., p. 382.

124 See for instance Muzafer Sherif, *Group Conflict and Cooperation*, Routledge, 1967.

125 John Roddam, 'Strangers in our Midst' in *The Observer*, 22 June, 1969; and J. H. Crook 'The Nature and Function of Territorial Aggression' in Ashley Montague, ed., *Man and Aggression*, OUP, 1968, pp. 141 f. See also: R. Ardrey, *The Territorial Imperative*, Atheneum, New York, 1966. Konrad Lorenz, *On Aggression*, Methuen, 1966; Desmond Morris, *The Naked Ape*, Jonathan Cape, 1967.

126 See K. Boulding in A. Montague, ed., *Man and Aggression*, op. cit.

127 See Charles Wagley and Marvin Harris, *Minorities in the New World*, Columbia University Press, 1958, especially 'Conclusion', pp. 237 ff.

128 See John Rex, 'Economic Aspects of Racism and Race Prejudice and the Urban Crisis, with special reference to the experience of Great Britain', UNESCO, 1969.

129 See John Rex, 'The Concept of Race in Sociological Theory';

and David Lockwood, 'Notes on Some Concepts of Race and Plural Society', papers delivered at the British Sociological Association Conference, March 1969.

130 See Ashley Montague, *Man's Most Dangerous Myth: The Fallacy of Race*, Meridian – The World Publishing Co., Cleveland and New York, 4th ed., 1965, pp. 151–2.

131 R. E. Park and E. W. Burgess, *Introduction to the Science o, Sociology*, University of Chicago Press, Chicago, Ill., 1921; and R. E. Park, *Collected Papers: Race and Culture*, Vol. I, 1950, and *Society*, Vol. III, 1958, The Free Press, Glencoe, Ill.

132 See John Rex, 'The Plural Society in Sociological Theory' in the *British Journal of Sociology*, X, 2 June 1959.

Bibliography

K. L. Little, 'Race and Society' in *The Race Question in Modern Science*, UNESCO, Paris, 1959.

K. L. Little, *Negroes in Britain*, Kegan Paul, 1948.

W. W. Daniel, *Racial Discrimination in England*, Penguin,1968.

Clifford S. Hill, *How Colour Prejudiced is Britain?*, Gollancz, 1965.

Ruth Glass, *Newcomers*, Allen & Unwin for Centre of Urban Studies, 1960.

Andrew Sharf, *The British Press and Jews under Nazi Rule*, OUP 1964.

Norman Cohn, *Warrant for Genocide*, Eyre and Spottiswoode, 1967.

The Political Quarterly, Vol. 39, No. 1., 1968.

Nicholas Deakin, ed., *Colour and the British Electorate*, Pall Mall, 1965.

Sheila Patterson, *Immigration and Race Relations in Britain 1960–67*, OUP, 1969.

James Parkes, *Antisemitism*, Vallentine Mitchell, 1963.

George Thayer, *The British Political Fringe*, Anthony Blond, 1968.

S. Collins, *Coloured Immigrants in Britain*, Lutterworth, 1967.

R. Desai, *Indian Immigrants in Britain*, OUP/IRR, 1963.

Mary Grigg, *The White Question*, Secker & Warburg, 1967.

G. E. Simpson and J. M. Yinger, *Racial and Cultural Minorities*, Harper & Row, 1965.

Gordon W. Allport, *The Nature of Prejudice*, Doubleday, New York, 1958.

Morris Ginsberg, 'On Prejudice' in *The Jewish Journal of Sociology*, Vol. 1, No. 1, 1959.

John Rex, 'The Plural Society in Sociological Theory' in *The British Journal of Sociology*, X, 2, 1959.

Ashley Montague ed., *Man and Aggression*, OUP, 1968.

Ashley Montague, *Man's Most Dangerous Myth*, Meridian, 1965.

Charles Wagley and Marvin Harris, *Minorities in the New World*, Columbia University Press, 1958.

R. E. Park and E. W. Burgess, *Introduction to the Science of Society*, University of Chicago Press, 1921.

CHAPTER 4

1 Sheila Patterson, *Dark Strangers*, Pelican, 1965, p. 61.
2 There is a great deal more material in this field than in that of demography.
3 J. A. Rex, 'The Sociology of a Zone of Transition' in R. E. Pahl (ed.), *Readings in Urban Sociology*, Pergamon Press, 1968.
4 E. J. B. Rose, *et al.*, op. cit., pp. 122–4.
5 Unpublished research papers of the British Universities Census Tracts Committee, E. Gittus, *et al.*, quoted in E. J. B. Rose, *et al.* op. cit., pp. 121, 147.
6 E. J. B. Rose, *et al.*, op. cit., p. 122.
7 R. B. Davison, *Black British*, IRR/OUP, 1966, p. 43.
8 E. J. B. Rose, *et al.*, op. cit., pp. 125–33.
9 Reproduced from: John Rex and Robert Moore, *Race, Community and Conflict*, IRR/OUP, 1967, p. 137.
10 See Robert Moore, 'Housing' in *Colour in Britain*, Richard Hooper, ed., BBC Publications, 1965, pp. 59, 71.
11 Sheila Patterson, op. cit., p. 55; and Elizabeth Burney, *Housing on Trial*, IRR/OUP, 1967, p. 162.
12 See above, p. 58
13 See E. J. B. Rose, op. cit., p. 236.
14 Rex and Moore, op. cit., p. 163.
15 See Martin Adeney in the *Guardian*, 26 Nov. 1969, p. 6.

16 See *Race Today*, Oct. 1969, p. iv., and the *Guardian*, 18 June, 1969.

17 See *The Times*, 31 Dec. 1969.

18 See *Race Today*, December 1969.

19 Elizabeth Burney, *Housing on Trial*, IRR/OUP, 1967, p. 188.

20 Lloyd P. Gartner, *The Jewish Immigrant in England, 1870–1914*, Allen & Unwin, 1959, pp. 147 f.

21 E. Krausz, *Leeds Jewry: Its History and Social Structure*, Heffers, Cambridge, 1964.

22 J. A. Jackson, *The Irish in Britain*, Routledge, 1963, pp. 43–6.

23 K. L. Little, *Negroes in Britain*, Kegan Paul, 1947, pp. 33 f; Sidney Collins, *Coloured Minorities in Britain*, Lutterworth Press, 1957.

24 See J. A. Rex, 'The Sociology of a Zone of Transition' in R. E. Pahl, op. cit.; and Davis McEntire, *Residence and Race*, University of California Press, Berkeley and Los Angeles, 1960. The European ghetto was in the late Middle Ages a clearly demarcated enclave, in some respects a corporate city-within-a-city, established voluntarily by Jews for their own protection, but gradually turning into an instrument for their oppression (See Charles Wagley and Marvin Harris, *Minorities in the New World*, Columbia University Press, 1958, p. 206). In much sociological literature the term has been used more broadly to describe a concentrated and highly segregated settlement of any minority group, although some have preferred to use the word 'quarter' in this context. Neither 'ghetto' nor 'quarter' is to be regarded as synonymous with 'slum' which is a generally applied term denoting an area of bad housing with a high concentration of social problems.

25 J. A. Rex, 'The Sociology of a Zone of Transition' in R. E. Pahl, ed., op. cit., p. 214.

26 ibid., p. 215.

27 See Sheila Patterson, *Dark Strangers*, Penguin, 1963, pp. 65 f.

28 E. J. B. Rose, op. cit., pp. 150 f.

29 E. Krausz, 'The Edgware Survey: Occupation and Social Class' in the *Jewish Journal of Sociology*, Vol. XI, No. 1, 1969, p. 76. The results of a survey in another part of London showed a similar difference; See A. Ziderman

'Teenage Survey' in *Jewish Journal of Sociology*, VIII, 2, 1966, p. 260.

30 R. B. Davison, *The Black British*, IRR/OUP, 1966, p. 68.

31 E. J. B. Rose, op. cit., p. 156.

32 See: 'G. P. Recruits' in *Pulse International*, 20.12.69.

33 Rose, op. cit., p. 157.

34 R. B. Davison, *Black British*, OUP/IRR, 1966, pp. 75 f; E.J.B. Rose, op. cit., p. 168. It may be the case that West Indians, like other minorities, e.g. the Jews, are rarely found in agriculture or mining because they have greater difficulty in being accepted in smaller, more closely-knit communities. The industrial city is more amenable in this respect.

35 Rose, op. cit., p. 169.

36 J. A. Jackson, *The Irish in Britain*, Routledge, 1963, pp. 97 f.

37 ibid., p. 106.

38 See V. D. Lipman, *A Social History of the Jews of England 1850–1940*, Watts, 1954; L. P. Gartner, *The Jewish Immigrant in England 1870–1914*, Allen & Unwin, 1959; N. Barou, *Jews in Work and Trade*, Trades Advisory Council, London, 1945.

39 E. Krausz 'Occupation and Social Advancement in Anglo-Jewry' in the *Jewish Journal of Sociology*, Vol. IV, No. 1, 1962, p. 85.

40 J. Zubrzycki, op. cit., p. 66.

41 E. J. B. Rose, op. cit., p. 173, Table 13.9.

42 Zubrzycki, op. cit., p. 67.

43 E. Krausz, 'The Edgware Survey: Occupation and Social Class', op. cit., p. 75.

44 Ng Kwee Choo, *The Chinese in London*, OUP/IRR, 1968, pp. 27–9. Kenneth L. Little, 'Race and Society' in *The Race Question in Modern Science*, UNESCO, 1956, p. 194.

45 J. A. Jackson, op. cit., p. 106.

46 See John Dearnley, 'Community Relations in Camden' in *Race Today*, February 1970, p. 41.

47 PEP *Planning*, Vol. XIV, No 268, 1947, p. 29.

48 PEP *Planning*, No. 259, 1946 quoted in Vol. XIV, No. 268, op. cit., p. 21.

49 See Institute of Race Relations, *Facts Paper – Colour and Immigration in the United Kingdom*, 1969, p. 16.

50 W. W. Daniel, *Racial Discrimination in England*, Penguin 1968, pp. 60, 100.

51 E. J. B. Rose, op. cit., p. 306.

52 See for instance the *Third Report by Commonwealth Immigrants Advisory Council*, Cmnd 2458, HMSO, 1964, p. 8.

53 See *CRC News*, October 1969.

54 See: *How the Race Relations Act Affects Personnel*, A Runnymede Trust Publication.

55 See *The Guardian*, 25 April 1967.

56 See, E. J. Mishan and L. Needleman, 'Immigration: Some Economic Effects' in *Lloyds Bank Review*, July 1966, especially p. 45; and by the same authors, 'Immigration: Long-Run Economic Effects' in *Lloyds Bank Review*, January 1968. See also E. J. Mishan, 'Does Immigration Confer Economic Benefits on the Host Country?' in *Economic Issues of Immigration*, The Institute of Economic Affairs, 1970.

57 See, Maurice Peston, 'Effects on the Economy', in E. J. B. Rose, *et al.*, op. cit., pp. 639 ff.; David Collard, 'Immigration and Discrimination: Some Economic Aspects' in *Economic Issues in Immigration*, op. cit., especially pp. 74 ff. For a fuller treatment of the subject see: K. Jones and A. D. Smith, *The Economic Impact of Commonwealth Immigration*, Cambridge University Press for The National Institute of Economic and Social Research, 1970; see also: *Commonwealth Immigration: The Economic Effects*, The Runnymede Trust, 1970.

58 *P.E.P. Report 1967*, in W. W. Daniel, op. cit., p. 133.

59 K. Jones, 'Immigrants and the Social Services' in the *National Institute Economic Review*, No. 41, August 1967, Table 6, p. 35.

60 E. J. B. Rose, op. cit., p. 325.

61 See *Race Today*, Feb. 1970, p. ii.

62 J. Zubrzycki, op. cit.

63 Sheila Patterson, *Immigrants in Industry*, OUP/IRR, 1968, p. 177.

64 ibid., p. 190.

65 See: 'Discrimination Against Jews in the Economic Field in Great Britain 1945–1955', a study prepared from its records by the Trades Advisory Council, London, January 1956, especially pp. 5–8; and a similar paper dated March 1958

(by courtesy of Mr M. Orbach, General Secretary of the Council).

66 W. W. Daniel, *Racial Discrimination in England*, op. cit.

67 Bob Hepple, *Race, Jobs and the Law in Britain*, Allen Lane, The Penguin Press, 1968, pp. 76–9.

68 See Sheila Patterson, *Immigration and Race Relations in Britain 1960–1967*, IRR/OUP, 1969, p. 167.

69 Adapted from: R. B. Davison, op. cit., Table 43, p. 89.

70 E. J. B. Rose, op. cit., p. 180.

71 It may be noted here that immigrants from the Old Commonwealth, e.g. Canada and Australia achieve on the whole a much better socio-economic position in this country than the English population. This is evident from the 1966 Census data.

72 Reproduced from: Peter L. Wright, *The Coloured Worker in British Industry*, OUP/IRR, 1968, p. 95.

73 Peter Collison, 'Immigrants' Varieties of Experience' in *New Society*, 26 June 1969.

74 Peter L. Wright, op. cit., pp. 214–17.

75 See: A. R. Truman, 'School' in *Colour in Britain*, Richard Hooper ed., BBC Publications, 1965, p. 99.

76 See: E. Krausz, *Leeds Jewry*, Heffer, Cambridge, 1964, p. 12.

77 See: V. D. Lipman, *Social History of the Jews in England*, Watts, 1954, p. 47.

78 See: E. J. B. Rose, op. cit., p. 267.

79 See: A. R. Truman, op. cit., p. 99.

80 E. J. B. Rose, op. cit., p. 176.

81 E. Krausz, 'The Edgware Survey: Occupation and Social Class' in The *Jewish Journal of Sociology*, Vol. XI, No. 1, 1969, p. 75.

82 J. W. Carrier, 'A Jewish Proletariat' in M. Mindlin and C. Bermant (eds.) *Explorations*, Barrie & Rockliff, 1967.

83 See: E. Krausz, 'The Economic and Social Structure of Anglo-Jewry' in Julius Gould and Shaul Esh (eds.) *Jewish Life in Modern Britain*, Routledge, 1964, p. 32; A. Ziderman, 'Leisure Activities of Jewish Teenagers in London', in the *Jewish Journal of Sociology*, Vol. VIII, No. 2, 1966.

84 Sheila Patterson, *Immigrants in Industry*, op. cit., p. 28.

85 J. A. Jackson, *The Irish in Britain*, op. cit., pp. 112–31.

86 E. J. B. Rose, op. cit., pp. 147, 181.

87 See Anthony Tucker, 'The facts and fancies about racial traits' in the *Guardian*, 14.4.69.

88 See L. C. Dunn and T. Dobzhansky, *Heredity, Race ana Society*, New American Library, 1952, p. 115; and Philip Mason 'Race: Some Myths and Realities' in E. J. B. Rose, op. cit., pp. 34 f.

89 See UNESCO Statement on Race, July 1950 quoted in Ashley Montague *Man's Most Dangerous Myth*, Meridian – The World Publishing Co., Cleveland N.Y., 4th ed., 1965, p. 362.

90 See UNESCO Statement on the Nature of Race and Race Differences, July 1952 quoted in Ashley Montague, op. cit., p. 370.

91 Michael Banton, *Race Relations*, Tavistock, 1967, pp. 53–4.

92 See P. E. Vernon, 'Intelligence' in J. Gould and W. D. Kolb, eds., *A Dictionary of the Social Sciences*, Tavistock, 1964, p. 340.

93 See Bryan Silcock, 'Race, Class and Brains' in the *Sunday Times Weekly Review*, 1.2.70, and 8.2.70; see also contributions by A. R. Jensen, M. Deutsch, A. L. Stinchcombe and others in the *Harvard Educational Review*, Vol. 39, Nos. 1, 2, 3, 1969.

94 See Robert Rosenthal and Leonore Jacobson, 'Self-Fulfilling Prophecies in the Classroom: Teachers' Expectations as Unintended Determinants of Pupils' Intellectual Competence' in M. Deutsch, I. Katz and A. R. Jensen, eds., *Social Class, Race and Psychological Development*, Holt, Rinehart and Winston, New York, 1968, pp. 219–53.

95 Maurice Freedman, *A Minority in Britain*, Vallentine-Mitchell, 1955, p. 201.

96 See Paul Vincent, 'The Measured Intelligence of Glasgow Jewish School-children' in the *Jewish Journal of Sociology*, Vol. VIII, No. 1, 1966, pp. 106–7

97 ibid.

98 See E. Krausz in Gould and Esh, op. cit., p. 33.

99 See above, Ch. 1.

100 Advisory Committee on Education – Community Relations Commission, *Education for a Multi-Cultural Society – 1. Syllabuses*, January 1970, p. 1; see also: 'Education for a Multi-Racial Society' in *CRC News*, Jan. 1970.

101 Bryan Silcock, op. cit.
102 See W. W. Daniel, *Racial Discrimination in England*, op. cit. and see above, p. 58.
103 Michael Banton, *Race Relations*, Tavistock, 1967, p. 393.
104 See R. E. Park, *Human Communities*, Collier-Macmillan, 1952, especially pp. 140–58.
105 John Rex, 'The Sociology of a Zone of Transition' in R. E. Pahl, ed., op. cit., p. 230.
106 John Rex and Robert Moore, *Race, Community and Conflict*, OUP/IRR, 1967, p. 11.
107 J. Milton Yinger, *A Minority Group in American Society*, McGraw Hill, New York, 1965, p. 112.
108 J. P. Fitzpatrick, 'The Adjustment of Puerto Ricans to New York City' in A. M. and C. B. Rose, eds., *Minority Problems*, Harper and Row, New York, 1965.
109 See: W. Lloyd Warner 'American Class and Caste', *American Journal of Sociology*, 42 (September 1936), p. 235; B. Benedict, 'Stratification in Plural Societies', *American Anthropologist*, 64 (1962), p. 1241.
110 See: W. Lloyd Warner, 'American Class and Caste', in the *American Journal of Sociology*, 42, September 1936, p. 235.
111 John Rex, 'The Sociology of a Zone of Transition', op. cit., p. 221.
112 See *CRC News*, November, 1969.
113 See *CRC News*, February, 1970.
114 Gunnar Myrdal, 'The Principle of Cumulation' in A. M. and C. B. Rose eds., *Minority Problems*, Harper & Row, New York, 1965, pp. 372–6.
115 ibid., p. 375.
116 John Rex, 'The Sociology of a Zone of Transition', op. cit., p. 231.

Bibliography

J. A. Rex, 'The Sociology of Zone of Transition' in R. E. Pahl, ed., *Readings in Urban Sociology*, Pergamon, 1968.
R. B. Davison, *Black British*, OUP/IRR, 1966.
Elizabeth Burney, *Housing on Trial*, OUP/IRR.

Davis McEntire, *Residence and Race*, University of California Press, Berkeley and Los Angeles, 1960.

Sheila Patterson, *Immigrants in Industry*, OUP/IRR, 1968.

Bob Hepple, *Race, Jobs and the Law in Britain*, Allen Lane, The Penguin Press, 1968.

Peter L. Wright, *The Coloured Worker in British Industry*, OUP/IRR, 1968.

L. C. Dunn and T. Dobzhansky, *Heredity, Race and Society*, New American Library, 1952.

The Harvard Educational Review, Vol. 39, Nos. 1, 2, and 3, 1969.

M. Deutsch, I. Katz, and A. R. Jensen, eds., *Social Class, Race and Psychological Development*, Holt, Rinehart and Winston, New York, 1968.

R. E. Park, *Human Communities*, Collier–MacMillan, 1952.

W. Lloyd Warner, 'American Class and Caste' in *American Journal of Sociology*, 42, 1936.

B. Benedict, 'Stratification in Plural Societies' in *American Anthropologist*, 64, 1962.

G. Franklin Edwards, ed., *E. Franklin Frazier on Race Relations*, University of Chicago Press, 1968.

J. Milton Yinger, *A Minority Group in American Society*, McGraw–Hill, New York, 1965.

A. M. and C. B. Rose, eds., *Minority Problems*, Harper & Row, New York, 1965.

CHAPTER 5

1 A paper on 'Race', using a wider comparative approach is being prepared by Michael Lyon for the comparability of data working party of the British Sociological Association.

2 See above, p. 10.

3 See above, p. 86.

4 R. A. Schermerhorn, *Comparative Ethnic Relations*, Random House, New York, 1970, p. 6.

5 R. E. Park and E. W. Burgess, *Introduction to the Science of Sociology*, University of Chicago Press, Chicago, 1921.

6 John Rex, 'Integration: The Reality' in *New Society*, 12 Aug. 1965.

7 See pp. 71 f.

8 J. Zubrzycki, *Polish Immigrants in Britain*, Nijhoff, The Hague, 1956; see also: Sheila Patterson 'Polish London' in *London* ed. by Centre for Urban Studies, MacGibbon & Kee, 1964, esp. pp. 331–5.

9 Zubrzycki, op. cit., p. 192, and J. L. Mills 'Britain's Community of Poles' in *New Society*, No. 42, 18.7.63, p. 13.

10 M. P. Banton, *The Coloured Quarter*, Jonathan Cape, 1955, p. 87.

11 See Zubrzycki, op. cit., p. 192; J. L. Mills, op. cit., and J. A. Jackson, *The Irish in Britain*, op. cit., p. 160.

12 See E. Krausz, 'The Edgware Survey: Factors in Jewish Identification, in the *Jewish Journal of Sociology*, Vol. XI, No. 2, Dec. 1969.

13 Louis Wirth 'The Problem of Minority Groups' in Ralph Linton, ed., *The Science of Man in the World Crisis*, Columbia University Press, New York, 1949.

14 See above pp. 74 f.

15 See R. E. Park and E. W. Burgess, *Introduction to the Science of Sociology*, University of Chicago Press, Chicago, 1921.

16 See: Sheila Patterson, *Dark Strangers*, Tavistock 1963; Sheila Patterson, *Immigrants in Industry*, op. cit.; Peter L. Wright, *The Coloured Worker in British Industry*, IRR/OUP, 1968; E. Krausz, 'The Edgware Survey; Occupation and Social Class' in the *Jewish Journal of Sociology*, Vol. XI, No. 1, June, 1969; R. B. Davison, *Black British*, OUP/IRR, 1966.

17 See above, pp. 59, 61.

18 Charles Price, 'The Study of Assimilation' in J. A. Jackson, ed., *Migration*, Cambridge University Press, 1969, p. 216.

19 N. Glazer and D. P. Moynihan, *Beyond the Melting Pot*, The MIT Press, 1963.

20 T. Shibutani and K. M. Kwan, *Ethnic Stratification*, Collier–Macmillan, 1965, p. 589.

21 David M. Heer, 'Negro-White Marriage in the United States' in *New Society*, 26 August 1965.

22 Michael Banton, *Race Relations*, Tavistock, 1967, p. 292.

23 R. A. Schermerhorn, op. cit., p. 15.

24 ibid., p. 13.

25 See Diana Spearman, 'Enoch Powell's Postbag' in *New Society*, 9 May 1968.

26 See M. Tumin's survey summarized in M. Banton, *Race Relations*, op. cit., pp. 389 f.

27 E. Krausz, 'The Edgware Survey: Factors in Jewish Identification', in the *Jewish Journal of Sociology*, Vol. XI, No. 2, Dec. 1969, pp. 161 f.

28 R. B. Davison, *Black British*, OUP/IRR, 1966, p. 125.

29 ibid.

30 J. Zubrzycki, op. cit., pp. 162 f.

31 See for instance: Ng Kwee Choo, *The Chinese in London*, OUP/IRR, 1966, p. 91.

32 See Lewis Nkosi, in the *Daily Telegraph Supplement*, 25 Nov. 1966.

33 See Katrin Fitzherbert, 'Immigrant Self-Help: The West Indians' in *New Society*, 13 March 1969; see also Ruth Glass, *Newcomers: West Indians in London*, Allen & Unwin for Centre for Urban Studies, 1960, pp. 96 ff.

34 E. V. Stonequist, *The Marginal Man*, Scribner's, New York, 1937.

35 J. A. Jackson, *The Irish in Britain*, op. cit., p. 159.

36 See R. E. L. Faris in Gould and Kolb, *A Dictionary of the Social Sciences*, op. cit., and F. M. Keesing, ibid., pp. 6 and 38; also M. Freedman, *A Minority in Britain*, op. cit., pp. 202, 227–240.

37 See: Anthony H. Richmond, 'Sociology of Migration in Industrial and Post-Industrial Societies', in J. A. Jackson, ed. *Migration*, op. cit., p. 251; see also: J. Zubrzycki, *Polish Immigrants in Britain*, op. cit., and E. Krausz, *Leeds Jewry*, op. cit.

38 John Rex and Robert Moore, *Race, Community and Conflict*, OUP/IRR, 1967, pp. 6, 7.

39 R. A. Schermerhorn, op. cit., p. 34.

40 H. M. Blalock, *Toward a Theory of Minority-Group Relations*, Wiley, New York, 1967, p. 110.

41 The re-analysis of the Survey of Race Relations suggests that the picture is more bleak than was originally thought and the view has been expressed that in relative terms the position of the West Indians in particular has been deteriorating. See:

Nicholas Deakin, *Colour, Citizenship and British Society*, Panther, 1970; and E. J. B. Rose 'Deteriorating Position of West Indians in Britain' in *The Times*, 15 May, 1970.

42 See Clifford Hill, *Immigration and Integration*, Pergamon, 1970, p. 202.

43 Examples: the inter-racial social clubs, some inter-faith bodies and certain welfare organizations.

44 John Rex, *Race Relations in Sociological Theory*, Weidenfeld and Nicolson, 1970, p. 110.

45 Pierre L. van den Berghe, 'Statement on Race and Conflict', paper read at the Fifth Annual Race Relations Conference, IRR, London, September, 1970.

46 Rex, op. cit., p. 104.

47 For a definition of 'urbanism' see J. Clyde Mitchell in P. Meadows and E. H. Mizruchi eds., *Urbanism, Urbanization and Change*, Addison–Wesley, 1969, p. 471.

48 (2) See R. E. Park and E. W. Burgess, *Introduction to the Science of Sociology*, University of Chicago Press, Chicago, 1921; and L. A. Coser, *The Functions of Social Conflict*, The Free Press, Glencoe, Ill., 1956.

49 (3) See Vincent Cable, 'Whither Kenyan Emigrants' in *Young Fabian Pamphlet*, No. 18, July 1969.

50 See E. Butterworth, 'Kenya Asians in Britain' in *Venture*, Vol. 20, No. 4, April, 1968, p. 23; see also: Michael Howard *et al.*, *The Greatest Claim*, Bow Group Pamphlet, July 1970.

51 See Paul Gottlieb, 'Social Mobility of the Jewish Immigrant', unpublished M.Phil., thesis, University of Nottingham, 1970.

52 See, for instance, the views of Mark Bonham-Carter, chairman of the Race Relations Board, reported in *The Guardian*, 14th Sept., 1970.

53 Michael Banton, 'Prejudice and Social Networks' in *The Jewish Journal of Sociology*, Vol. VII, No. 1, June 1965, p. 112; and see: Robin M. Williams, *Strangers Next Door: Ethnic Relations in American Communities*, Prentice-Hall, Englewood Cliffs, New Jersey, 1964, pp. 54, 179.

54 Chaim Bermant, *Troubled Eden: An Anatomy of British Jewry*, Vallentine Mitchell, 1969, p. 257.

55 A. H. Halsey, 'Race Relations: The Lines To Think On' in *New Society*, No. 390, 19th March, 1970, p. 473; and see:

John Goldthorpe, 'Social Inequality and Social Integration in Britain' in *Advancement of Science*, Dec. 1969; W. G. Runciman, *Relative Deprivation and Social Justice*, Routledge, 1966.

56 See Bernard Barber, 'Social Stratification' in *International Encyclopedia of the Social Sciences*, Crowell–Collier Macmillan, 1968, pp. 289 ff.

57 Charles Wagley and Marvin Harris, *Minorities in the New World*, Columbia University Press, New York, 1958, p. 295.

I have attempted in this chapter to present an analysis by means of sociological theories, which I tried to state in concise form and to buttress by means of definitions adopted for a number of key terms. Despite this, I am aware that I may have assumed familiarity with such theories on the part of the reader which is not entirely warranted. The following short bibliography is intended to correct this and to encourage the reader to pursue a deeper approach to ethnic relations. It is also the case that the chapter is based on wider material than that suggested by the notes. I am including, therefore, in the bibliography, besides the general sociological works, a number of books and articles, concerned specifically with ethnic relations, which merit further attention.

Bibliography

Robert K. Merton, *Social Theory and Social Structure*, The Free Press, Glencoe, Ill., 1957.

John Rex, *Key Problems of Sociological Theory*, Routledge & Kegan Paul, 1961.

Lewis A. Coser, *Continuities in the Study of Social Conflict*, The Free Press, New York, 1967.

Gerhard Lenski, *Power and Privilege*, McGraw Hill, New York, 1960.

S. N. Eisenstadt, *The Absorption of Immigrants*, Routledge, 1954.

G. Myrdal, *An American Dilemma*, Harper, New York, 1944.

Philip Mason, *Patterns of Dominance*, Oxford University Press, 1970.

F. Barth ed., *Ethnic Groups and Boundaries*, Allen & Unwin, 1969.

Milton M. Gordon, *Assimilation in American Life*, Oxford University Press, 1964.

E. F. Frazier, *The Negro in the United States*, Macmillan, New York 1949.

O. C. Cox, *Caste, Class and Race*, Doubleday, New York, 1948.

Everett C. Hughes, 'Race Relations and the Sociological Imagination' in *American Sociological Review*, 28 (December 1963).

M. G. Smith, *The Plural Society in the British West Indies*, University of California Press, Berkeley and Los Angeles, 1965.

S. M. Elkins, *Slavery*, University of Chicago Press, Chicago, 1959.

'Colour and Race' issue in *Daedalus*, Journal of the American Academy of Arts and Sciences, Spring 1967.

Man, Race and Darwin, papers read at the joint conference of the Royal Anthropological Institute and the Institute of Race Relations, Oxford University Press, 1960.

D. V. Glass, ed., 'Introduction' to *Cultural Assimilation of Immigrants*, Population Studies Supplement, March, 1950.

Percy S. Cohen, 'The Study of Immigrants' in *The Jewish Journal of Sociology*, Vol. VII, No. 2, (December 1965).

W. D. Borrie, *Cultural Integration of Immigrants*, UNESCO, Paris, 1959.

M. Tumin, *Comparative Perspectives on Race Relations*, Little Brown, New York, 1969.

John Rex, *Race Relations in Sociological Theory*, Weidenfeld & Nicolson, London, 1970.

R. A. Schermerhorn, *Comparative Ethnic Relations*, Random House, New York, 1970.

Index

Immigrants, 34 ff; *see also* Commonwealth Immigrants Acts
Immigration Control Associations, 70
'Indenture' system, 13
Indian Workers' Association, 72, 75
Indians, 17 f, 35 ff
Industrial distribution, 97
Industrial society, 87; *see also* Urbanism
In-group – out-group comparisons, 83 f
Integration 130; *see also* Pluralistic integration
Intelligence, distribution of 116; *see also* Heredity
Intermarriage, 59–61, 127, 130
Internal economies, of minorities, 102
International Friendship Organizations, 67
Irish, the, 22 f, 30, 34, 55, 73 f
    nationalism of, 74, 132, 154 (n. 93)
Irish Self-determination League, 72
Italians, 35

Jackson, J. A., 23, 30, 32, 74, 99, 127 ff
Jacobson, L., 116
Jati, 19
Jewish Chronicle, 113
Jews, the, 24 f, 30, 35, 56 f, 72 f; *see also* Ashkenazi, Oriental, Sephardi Jews
Jones, Philip, 11
Judaism, 125, 128

Kelsall, R. K., 53
Kenya Asians, 137 f
Kinship ties, 125
    among Indians and Pakistanis, 18 f
    among the Irish, 24
    among Jews, 26
    among the West Indians, 14 f
Krausz, E., 147 (n. 36)

Labour Party, 62, 65 f, 78
Latvians, 28, 35
Leeds Poale Zion, 73
Liberals, 62
Lipman, V. D., 56
Lithuanians, 28, 35

Little, K. L., 58
Locating minority populations, *see* Krausz, E.
London dockers, the, 65

McCarran Act, 14
Majority, the, *see* Dominant group
Marginal man/personality, 132
Marranos, 25
Marriage rate, 47
Marxists, 73, 131
Mason, Philip, 75
'Melting pot', the, 128
Migration 55; *see also* 'Chain migration'
Militant/militancy, 68–75, 122, 126 f
Milner-Holland Report, 90
Minority:
    definitions of, 10, 123, 136
    identification by members of, 125 f, 129
    size of groups, 36 f
    see also Locating minority populations
Muslim religion, 17, 20; *see also* Black Muslims
Myrdal, Gunnar, 122

National Committee against Racial Discrimination, 67
National Committee for Commonwealth Immigrants, 67, 79
National Socialist Movement, 69
Nationalism, 73
Nazism, 26, 61, 63 f, 69 f, 82
'Negritude', 131
Negroes, 14, 16, 120, 128 ff, 131
Negroid, 18
New Zealanders, 45
Nkosi, Lewis, 131

Observer, 64
Occupations, *see* Employment
Oi T'ung Association, 71
Orange Associations, 68
Oriental Jews, 137 f
Overcrowding, 56, 92

Pakistanis, 17 f, 35 ff
Park, R. E., 118, 124
Parkes, James, 69
Patterson, Sheila, 66, 90, 108, 114